Automated Busines

Build a Massive Community

and Scale Your Business with

Heart-Centered Marketing.

How to design and implement sales and marketing automation that is both efficient and nurturing, and build a loyal community of engaged customers without losing the personal touch.

Tina Brinkley Potts LLC

 386 Walmart Drive, Suite 7 #39, Camden, DE 19934

support@tinabrinkleypotts.com

302-208-8844

guide. All links are for information purposes only and are not warranted for content, accuracy, or any other implied or explicit purpose.

Earnings Disclaimer: All income examples in this book are just that – examples. They are not intended to represent or guarantee that everyone will achieve the same results. You understand that each individual's success will be determined by his or her desire, dedication, background, effort, and motivation to work. There is no guarantee you will duplicate any of the results stated here. You recognize any business endeavor has inherent risk for loss of capital.

"The typical result one can expect to achieve is nothing. The "typical" person never gets to the end of this book. The "typical" person fails to implement anything. Thus they earn nothing. Zero. No income. And perhaps a loss of income. That's because "typical" people do nothing and therefore they achieve nothing. Be atypical. Do something. Implement something. If it doesn't work; make a change...and implement that. Try again...try harder. Persist. And reap the rewards."

Acknowledgements

Expressing gratitude to the myriad individuals who have played a role in my life and business journey is a task too vast for words. To everyone who has contributed, supported, and believed in me – your love and appreciation resonate deeply.

Dad, your early encouragement with computers sculpted my path, teaching me the power of being different. In a world where tech prowess for a young black girl wasn't the norm, you instilled in me the courage to stand out. Your influence accompanies me every day.

To Jeremy, my standout ally at Keap, your unwavering support fuels my passion. Together, let's propel countless businesses toward building their automated empires. Cheers to growth and collaboration!

Preface

"To be yourself in a world that is constantly trying to make you something else is the greatest accomplishment." – Ralph Waldo Emerson

Imagine stepping into a world where the thrill of growth meets the authenticity of heart-centered connections. This book is a carefully curated journey, one that answers the poignant call for entrepreneurs and business owners who are wrestling with the paradox of scaling their businesses without compromising the essence of personal engagement. The pages within are a testament to the possibility that efficiency and warmth can exist in harmonious balance, where automated strategies and nurturing relationships are not antithetical but synergistic.

In the pursuit of efficiency, it's all too easy to lose sight of the human element that makes businesses flourish. It's a dance of delicate balance – infusing automation into your marketing and sales processes while still sparking the kind of genuine connection that turns casual browsers into lifelong advocates. As someone who has woven the fabric of my professional life out of helping others magnify their impact, I recognized a striking need: a comprehensive guide that not only streamlined automation but did so with a reverent nod to the nuanced demands of the human heart.

Throughout my journey, I've witnessed a colorful spectrum of personal experiences with undeniable parallels. Picture Sarah, a passionate small business owner whose lively spirit once suffused every customer interaction. As her business burgeoned, her sparkle dimmed under the weight of unsustainable manual processes. Then there's Michael, the innovative tech startup founder whose groundbreaking ideas were lost in a quagmire of impersonal autoresponders and generic sales funnels. Each story echoed a mutual refrain: automation's cold touch diluting the vibrant warmth once felt in their enterprises.

These narratives were the clarion call that led to the creation of this book. It's where I've distilled the wisdom gained from a mosaic of global endeavors, from assisting everyday experts to working with recognized celebrities – each seeking to leverage their unique voice in a digital symphony that often feels dissonant.

My heartfelt thanks extend to the mentors and peers who've illuminated my path – from the vibrant minds at Momentum, who empowered me to elevate my vision, to the myriad clients and colleagues who shared their vibrant stories of struggle and triumph. Their support and insights have been the guideposts in this expedition of crafting a book that is as much a roadmap as it is a mirror reflecting the collective aspirations of enterprising spirits.

Before we dive into the details, take a moment of appreciation for the choice you've made to join me on this odyssey. Your time and trust are not taken lightly, and it gives me immense joy to know that you are here, poised at the threshold of transformation.

This book is penned for you – the driving forces of innovation, the creators of opportunity, the curators of community. You needn't be a programmer or steeped in technical lingo, for this is crafted to be your guide, irrespective of where you are in your entrepreneurial odyssey.

In the chapters ahead, we will traverse the gamut from automating customer interactions to cultivating a thriving online community. With each word, I aim to invoke a spark of clarity and confidence. Thank you for choosing this path, and I invite you to turn the page, to begin unearthing the secrets to scaling your empire with precision, passion, and profound connection. Let's embark on a voyage where every automated system thrums with the heartbeat of your brand, and each customer feels the touch of your care, miles apart yet closer than ever.

Before you turn the page, I want to invite you to take the course I specifically designed to go with this book called The Fundamentals of an Automated Business Empire. This course normally sells at $997 but you can get the course for $97 by entering promo code **ABEBOOK**.

https://bit.ly/ABEFundamentals

Introduction

In this introduction, I want to make it clear why you should even consider reading this book.

Inside these pages, you'll discover strategies that transcend time, proven effective through years of implementation with my clients. The results are undeniable, generating over $250 million in revenue, not to mention the countless hours saved and operational efficiencies gained.

Embrace technology with open arms; it's not a hassle but a powerful ally. My journey with technology began in sixth grade, programming with ones and zeros. It's evolved into a tool that deepens relationships, allows for lasting connections, and enhances my role as a mother.

Let me take you back to a defining moment - an unexpected award in computer class, a memory cherished with my late father. Now, with both parents gone, technology keeps me connected to extended family, turning what some see as the devil (social media) into a lifeline of support.

Reflect on your own life. Have you ever felt present yet absent, caught in the perpetual cycle of work and obligations? I've been there. But with technology and strategic automation, I've reclaimed my time, ensuring my business thrives even as I sleep.

For a long time, my motto was hustle plus automation equals empire. Now, I simply say: Automation supports my life and business the way I want to live it:

Fully present with my family instead of worrying about money.

Chapter 1: Balancing Efficiency and Genuine Care

"The true art lies in the subtleties – the instances where you pause the machinery to personally reach out or tailor your automated responses to feel unexpectedly human."

In the arid embrace of a converted warehouse, Amber's fingers danced across the keyboard with the kind of mechanical precision that accompanies years of repetition. Screens glowing, data flowing; this was her domain—efficient, productive, automated. Yet, the cogitation of efficiency could not drown out the whispering question of warmth in her business.

She remembered, not long ago, how a handwritten note tucked into a package had drawn a deluge of appreciation from a customer. The dichotomy of the modern marketplace: a yearning for the bygone days of personal touch against the relentless ticking of the digital clock.

Drawn from her reverie by the vibration of a notification, Amber observed a customer's tweet praising the support bot's swift response—therein lied the rub. Her clientele sought the expediency her automation provided but craved the heartbeat of human connection. How should one marry the instantaneous to the intimate?

A colleague, Max, sidelined by Amber's screen, spoke of the recent webinar, where they underlined the art—no, the necessity—of balancing this very paradox. "It's all about personalization, at scale," he said, borrowing the phrase from the presenter, "You design the automation, but you infuse it with the empathy of a handwritten letter."

Amber knew the truth of Max's paraphrases and wondered at the practicality of personalizing automated messages without sacrificing authenticity. The coffee mug emblazoned with 'To Humanize is to Personalize' caught the corner of her eye, its contents long cooled—a testament to the day's unyielding momentum.

She pondered the solution while walking home through the spine-chilling squeal of a fast-moving maglev overhead, the cold concrete of the city's tech quarter. Could technology adapt to recognize the subtlety of human sentiment? Could algorithms learn empathy?

Inside, Amber mapped out a vision where each email her company sent was forged by machine efficiency but bore the mark of human craft, each support ticket closed with the finesse of genuine care. The daunting challenge excited her—an orchestra of code and emotion playing in harmony.

Where does one draw the line between the intimacy of the handcrafted and the efficiency of the automated? How does one distill human care into bytes and data streams?

The Art of Connection in the Age of Automation

Harnessing the dual engines of efficiency and genuine care is not an easy task in the modern business landscape. As we stand on the brink of a new era where technology can handle tasks at the speed of thought, a paradox emerges: How do we retain that invaluable human touch? **This chapter is the cornerstone of creating a business model that not only thrives on automation but also flourishes with a heart**. It will guide you through understanding the subtle alchemy of combining the precision of technology with the warmth of human interaction to build an empire of loyal customers and devoted community members.

At the core of every successful business are relationships; bonds with customers that go beyond transactions. While automation has the capacity to handle various aspects of your business, it runs the risk of sterilizing customer experiences. Here, you'll learn to weave a tapestry of personal connection into the fabric of automated systems effectively. It's about **designing automated processes that feel personal and creating marketing strategies that resonate on a human level**.

Strategies for Synergy

Knowing how to balance these two pillars will set the foundation for your journey towards sustainable growth. The readers will delve into the strategies that preserve the essence of your brand's message while delivering it through the most efficient conduits. **Understanding the nuances of communication and ensuring that every automated interaction has a touch of personalization is crucial.** By implementing these tactics, a seamless synergy between automation and genuine care is achievable.

The Architects of Engagement

In this voyage of blending heart with efficiency, we will explore the role of technology as the architect of engagement. Automation, when executed well, offers a consistent, dependable structure upon which to build profound human connections. Yet, the true art lies in the subtleties – *the instances where you pause the machinery to personally reach out or tailor your automated responses to feel unexpectedly human*. This chapter is your blueprint, detailing the intricacies of creating a system that supports genuine customer engagement, nurturing leads, and driving brand loyalty without losing the essence of who you are as a business.

Loyal Communities and Growth Metrics

As we delve deeper, one key aspect will be how to measure the impact of this balance on your business. *Setting goals, tracking progress, and measuring success* are part of the fabric of effective automation and genuine care. Learning to utilize data to refine your approach, while also listening to the stories beyond numbers, will arm you with the knowledge to grow your empire without sacrificing the quality of each customer's journey.

The Human Element

The art of balancing efficiency with genuine care can be the difference between a forgettable interaction and a memorable experience that fosters a lasting customer relationship. Strategies that propagate sustainable growth and customer loyalty are not just about getting the job done; they're designed to leave a lasting impression—a sense of care and attention that resonates with your audience. You'll discover how to inject the *human element* into every automated process, ensuring that your brand isn't just seen, but felt.

As we progress through the twists and turns of building your Automated Business Empire, let's remember that the heart of your business lies in this balance. Embrace the technology that helps you grow, but never lose sight of the humans you serve. This chapter sets the stage for the rest of your journey, equipping you with the foundational principles that will empower you to not just scale, but to soar with a community-centric approach.

Embracing a balance of efficiency and genuine care is essential for nurturing automation and heart-centered marketing. While automation streamlines processes and saves time, genuine care and nurturing are essential for building strong relationships with customers. Balancing the two allows for efficient processes while maintaining a personal connection with the audience, leading to sustainable growth and customer loyalty.

Balancing Automation Efficiency with Genuine Care

It's important to recognize that automation is a powerful tool for increasing productivity and optimizing processes. Automation allows you to streamline repetitive tasks, maximize efficiency, and allocate more time and resources to activities that require genuine care and personal touch. However, it's equally crucial to understand that genuine care and empathy are the building blocks of strong, lasting relationships with your customers. Without these, automation can come off as cold and robotic, alienating your audience rather than connecting with them on a personal level.

When seeking to achieve this balance, it's essential to view automation not as a replacement for human interaction, but as a means to enhance it. By automating routine processes, you free up time to engage with your audience in a more personal and meaningful way. This synergy between automation and genuine care allows you to foster stronger connections, provide tailored experiences, and ultimately build a loyal community of engaged customers.

Understanding the Dynamics

Efficiency and genuine care are not opposing forces; rather, they are complementary aspects of a successful customer relationship strategy. Efficiency ensures that your business operates smoothly and optimally, while genuine care ensures that your customers feel valued, heard, and understood. It's a delicate balance that, when achieved, results in customer satisfaction, loyalty, and advocacy.

By understanding the importance of balancing automation efficiency with genuine care, you position your business to thrive in a competitive market. The key is to recognize the value of each element and the pivotal role they play in nurturing sustainable growth and cultivating customer loyalty. As you move forward in implementing this balanced approach, remember that both efficiency and genuine care are essential for creating a community of loyal and engaged customers.

It's crucial for your business to embrace both elements in order to not only meet the needs of your audience but also exceed their expectations. This strategy creates a competitive advantage as it builds a foundation of trust and appreciation that is hard to replicate. With this understanding, you can streamline processes while maintaining a personal connection with your audience, ultimately leading to lasting success and growth.

The art of balancing automation and genuine care is the key to unlocking sustainable growth and long-term customer loyalty. Keep reading to learn how to streamline processes while maintaining a personal connection with your audience.

In today's fast-paced digital landscape, striking a balance between efficiency and genuine care is crucial for successful marketing and sales automation. It's essential to streamline processes while still maintaining a personal connection with your audience. By achieving this balance, you can nurture strong customer relationships, leading to sustainable growth and customer loyalty.

To streamline processes without sacrificing personal connection, it's important to **utilize automation tools** strategically. Implementing marketing automation software can significantly streamline repetitive tasks, such as email marketing, lead scoring, and social media management. These tools allow you to reach a wider audience while still maintaining a personalized touch. Likewise, CRM (customer relationship management) systems can centralize customer data, enabling you to tailor your communications based on individual preferences and behaviors.

While automation can optimize your operations, it's equally crucial to **infuse every interaction with a genuine sense of care**. Take the time to craft personalized messages, respond to customer inquiries promptly, and show appreciation for your audience's support. *Remember, behind every data point and email address is a real person with unique needs and desires.* By acknowledging and addressing these individual differences, you can develop a stronger connection with your audience.

As you strive for efficiency, don't overlook the significance of **genuine human connection**. Personalized experiences, such as celebrating customer milestones or sending personalized recommendations, can foster emotional connections that go beyond transactional interactions. Furthermore, hosting live Q&A sessions, webinars, or virtual events can provide opportunities for real-time, interactive engagement, creating a sense of community and belonging.

Balancing efficiency and genuine care also requires **consistent monitoring and refinement**. Regularly evaluate your automation strategies to ensure they align with your audience's expectations and preferences. Use analytics tools to track customer engagement and behavior, gathering insights to refine your approach and deliver more targeted, relevant content. By remaining agile and adaptable, you can continuously nurture your customer relationships while optimizing your automation processes.

It's important to remember that while automation can save time and boost efficiency, it should serve as a tool to enhance your ability to provide **personalized care**. Ultimately, by striking a balance between automation and personalization, you can build a loyal community of engaged customers while scaling your business effectively.

In the next section, we'll explore specific **strategies for nurturing sustainable growth** and fostering customer loyalty through this balanced approach.

As you harness the power of automation, it's critical to understand that the heart of your business is not the technology itself, but the lasting relationships you build with your customers. **Automation can scale efforts**, but only genuine care can deepen customer loyalty. This is not a trade-off but a **synergy** that, when applied effectively, nurtures sustainable growth. How can you strike that balance? Here are transformative strategies that interweave automation's prowess with the touch of human empathy.

Automate with Personalization at the Core

Begin by personalizing your automated communications. Irrespective of how advanced your systems are, **personalization** is the bridge that connects efficiency to empathy. Utilize customer data to tailor messages that resonate with specific segments of your audience. By doing so, your business isn't just sending out information; it is speaking directly to the individual needs and desires of each customer. Whether through email campaigns or social media interactions, add a personal touch to make each communication feel one-on-one, even when it's automated.

Foster Relationships with Regular Engagement

Automation should not be a set-it-and-forget-it tool. Inject life into your marketing by regularly reviewing and optimizing automated sequences. It's worth setting up triggers based on customer actions that initiate personalized automated responses. This ensures that customers feel acknowledged and valued, not just as part of a marketing database, but as individuals with unique preferences and behaviors. Pairing this strategy with periodic **human follow-ups** can turn routine transactions into meaningful interactions, strengthening the customer bond.

Empower Through Educational Content

Offer value beyond your product or service by sharing educational content that helps your customers solve problems or improve their lives. Use automated systems to deliver helpful guides, tutorials, or thought leadership articles tailored to where each customer is in their lifecycle. By positioning your brand as a resource, not just a commodity, you establish a **relationship rooted in trust and value**.

Use Feedback Loops to Enhance Care

Incorporate automated surveys and feedback requests at different touchpoints to show customers that their opinions matter. Actively listen to their experiences and use the insights to refine your approach. This continuous feedback loop can be automated, but *response to the feedback* should be personal and attentive, fostering a culture of improvement and attentiveness.

Leverage Data for Meaningful Insights

Thoroughly analyze the data gathered by your automated systems. Understand customer behaviors, preferences, and pain points. Arm yourself with these insights to deliver more effective marketing messages and product solutions. This strategic use of data ensures that your automated efforts are always grounded in customer-centric thinking, making efficiency feel more like genuine care.

Surprise and Delight Strategically

Automate unexpected gestures of appreciation. Whether it's a birthday discount code, an anniversary recognition, or a reward for customer loyalty, these can be systematized to surprise and delight customers at scale. However, the selection of these moments should be thoughtful, making the customer feel truly special. It's not the automation that will be remembered, but the *feeling of being uniquely valued*.

Reflect and Adjust for Improvement

Regularly take time to assess the balance between your automated systems and the level of personal care provided. Collect input from your team and customers about what's working and what could be better. Agile adjustments to your automation can lead to significant improvements in customer experience. Such reflection should be a scheduled part of your strategy, ensuring that automation serves the customer relationship rather than overshadowing it.

These strategies are not endpoints but starting points for a journey where efficiency and genuine care coalesce. By implementing these approaches thoughtfully, entrepreneurs can maintain a thriving and loyal customer base that feels as connected to your brand as you are to your mission. Remember, in the world of marketing, **automation should amplify your reach, but genuine care will amplify your impact**.

In this chapter, we've delved into the crucial concept of balancing efficiency and genuine care in the realm of heart-centered marketing and automation. **Embracing this balance forms the foundation for nurturing automation effectively and sets the stage for building long-lasting relationships with your audience.**

Throughout the chapter, we've discussed the significance of understanding the importance of this equilibrium, learning how to streamline processes while maintaining a personal touch, and discovering strategies for nurturing sustainable growth and customer loyalty through balanced automation and genuine care. **These insights serve as a solid groundwork for implementing tangible changes in your marketing and sales strategies, leading to meaningful**

results.

Imagine the thrill of witnessing a community of engaged customers growing around your business, empowered by the efficiency of automation and enriched by your genuine care and personal connection. Picture the satisfaction of seeing your business scale new heights while retaining the core values that define your brand. **All of this, and more, awaits as you continue to explore the transformative concepts laid out in this book.**

Stay tuned for the upcoming chapters, where we'll dive even deeper into practical strategies and actionable steps to help you achieve your goal of building a massive community and scaling your business with heart-centered marketing. The journey has just begun, and the rewards are waiting for those who are ready to seize them.

Chapter 2: Behavior-Based Marketing for Personalized Automation

*"**Behavior-based marketing** is not merely a strategy; it's an intimate dance with data that, when understood, allows you to lead your audience through a story arch crafted just for them."*

The sun had already dipped below the horizon when James turned on his desk lamp, bathing his workspace in a warm glow against the darkening sky. He sat back in his chair, eyes tired from the computer screen, his mind a whirlpool of marketing strategies and consumer behaviors yet to be deciphered. James knew that the success of his latest campaign hinged on unlocking the intricacies of personalized automation sequences. Today, his company was at the precipice, looking down into the valley of unfathomable potential that lay in behavior-based marketing.

Each click, each opened email, and each abandoned cart told a story—a narrative James was determined to understand and translate into an actionable strategy. The soothing aroma of coffee filled the air, a sensory lifeboat amidst the sea of data points and analytics. As he sipped the dark brew, James considered the individual behind every statistic: the stay-at-home parent browsing on a smartphone, the young professional comparing prices during a lunch break. These were not merely numbers but people, each with distinct tastes, needs, and timelines.

The clock ticked steadily, marking the passage of time as James crafted a new marketing sequence, one that felt intuitive, almost a natural conversation rather than a robotic script. He wove personalization into the very fabric of his automation, targeting not just demographics but behaviors and preferences. With every decision, the campaign morphed into something more resonant, a mirror reflecting back the customer's own desires and inclinations.

A soft chime from his computer heralded the arrival of fresh data—a sign that his deployed tests were trickling in results. Each notification was like a pulse, an affirmation that resonance was not only possible but within reach. He imagined a graph, with each upward tick representing a real human connection made, an engagement inspired by understanding and empathy. This was marketing with a soul, and James felt it deeply.

Outside, the city buzzed with life, people moving within the web of lights as unknown constellations. The day had been long, and the evening promised no reprieve, yet James was alight with the thrill of challenge. As the stars crystallized above, unblinking in the vast ocean of the night sky, one question lingered in the air, a thought that cut to the core of his quest: Would this deeper understanding of human behavior finally bridge the gap between a company's message and its audience's heart?

Unlock the Potential of Every Click

Every interaction online is a whisper of data calling out, revealing a unique story—what leads individuals to engage, stay, or depart. Discerning these digital narratives is essential, not just to connect, but to craft a journey that feels personal and enthralling for each visitor. **Behavior-based marketing** is not merely a strategy; it's an intimate dance with data that, when understood, allows you to lead your audience through a story arch crafted just for them. It is here, in the granularity of actions and preferences, that you can tailor marketing efforts with unmatched precision.

In an age where automation has become the bedrock of scaling businesses, the human element remains irreplaceable. The art lies in blending the efficiency of automation with the authenticity of personalization. Your audience's behaviors are breadcrumbs that lead you to **the heart of their desires**, unveiling what they seek and how they want to be approached. Leverage this knowledge, and you convert faceless automation into a personal touchpoint that nurtures leads and galvanizes your community.

The impact of personalized automation sequences is staggering—they transform the impersonal to the intimate, elevating each exchange from noise in the ether to resonant communication. Customers feel seen, understood, and valued. The effect? **Deeper engagement**, heightened loyalty, and a robust bottom line. To implement this strategy effectively, you must become fluent in the language of consumer behavior, interpreting clicks and pauses as clear indications of preference.

Delving deeper, behavior-based marketing not only reveals what to offer but also when to extend that offer for maximum receptivity. Timing is pivotal, acting as the secret ingredient that turns interest into action. Recognizing the *right moment* to present a solution can mean the difference between a recurring customer and a lost opportunity. With precise behavior analysis, automation becomes a synchronized orchestra playing to the rhythm of your audience's heartbeats.

Yet, all this data and insight are meaningless without action. Thus, the focus of our journey here is actionable brilliance. This chapter empowers you with concrete steps to transform raw data into robust, personalized campaigns. You will learn how small adjustments based on behavior analysis can usher in a **dramatic shift** in the effectiveness of your marketing efforts. This isn't about data for data's sake; it's about fostering real connections at scale—connections that fuel both your community's spirit and your business's growth.

Embrace the Power of Individuality

To excel, you'll master a dual focus: understanding individual behaviors and recognizing patterns at scale. This adeptness allows you to construct automation that speaks directly to the individual while echoing throughout the community. Through this lens, the breadth and depth of personalization play out in endless combinations, **tailoring experiences** that resonate widely yet feel immensely personal.

Walking this path, you'll tap into a treasure trove of results-focused strategies. Expect to begin drawing a roadmap of **behavioral triggers** and harnessing modern tools to transform these insights into potent, automated workflows. Prepare to see a marked evolution in your engagement metrics as you apply these principles, crafting campaigns that align closely with the desires and behaviors of your audience.

Maintain an upbeat tempo, for you are crafting more than campaigns; you're sewing the very fabric of a vibrant, engaged community.

Personalized automation is the thread that strengthens the bonds within this tapestry, and behavior-based marketing is the pattern that emerges, intricate and telling. Armed with the strategies from this chapter, you stand ready to ignite a marketing transformation—one that scales, connects, and endures.

Understanding the behaviors and preferences of your audience is the cornerstone of creating a successful and effective marketing strategy. By recognizing the significance of understanding audience behaviors and preferences, you can tailor your marketing efforts to meet their specific needs and interests. This personalized approach enhances the effectiveness of automation by resonating with the audience on a deeper level, ultimately leading to increased engagement, conversions, and brand loyalty.

When you take the time to understand your audience's behaviors and preferences, you gain valuable insights into what resonates with them, what motivates them to take action, and what drives their decision-making process. This knowledge allows you to create targeted and personalized marketing campaigns that speak directly to their needs and desires. By tailoring your messages to align with their preferences, you can capture their attention and build a deeper connection with them.

By leveraging behavior-based marketing, you can:

- *Create personalized messaging*: Tailoring your marketing

messages based on your audience's behaviors and preferences allows you to speak directly to their needs and interests, making your communication more relevant and engaging.

- *Drive targeted actions*: Understanding your audience's behaviors enables you to prompt specific actions at strategic moments, leading to higher engagement and conversion rates.
- *Build stronger relationships*: When you show your audience that you understand and appreciate their preferences, you build trust and rapport, fostering long-term relationships and brand loyalty.

Moreover, behavior-based marketing enables you to identify patterns and trends within your audience's engagement, enabling you to refine and optimize your campaigns for maximum impact. This data-driven approach ensures that your marketing efforts are consistently effective and efficient, producing measurable results that contribute to the growth and success of your business.

Ultimately, by tailoring your marketing efforts to align with the behaviors and preferences of your audience, you can:

- *Cultivate a more meaningful connection*: Connecting with your audience on a personal level, demonstrating that you understand and value their preferences, lays the foundation for a strong and lasting connection.
- *Enhance the relevance of your messaging*: Delivering content and offers that are tailored to your audience's behaviors and preferences increases the relevance of your marketing, leading to

higher engagement and response rates.

- *Strengthen brand loyalty:* When your audience feels understood, appreciated, and catered to, they are more likely to develop a sense of loyalty and advocacy for your brand.

Let's explore how behavior-based marketing enhances the effectiveness of automation by resonating with the audience on a deeper level.

Behavior-based marketing enhances the effectiveness of automation by creating a deeper connection with the audience. Understanding the behaviors and preferences of the audience allows for tailored marketing efforts that resonate on a personal level. By leveraging behavior-based insights, businesses can craft targeted automation sequences that deliver the right message to the right people at the right time. This personalized approach is essential for cultivating meaningful relationships with leads and customers, leading to increased engagement and loyalty.

By analyzing audience behavior, businesses gain valuable insights into the preferences, interests, and buying patterns of their target market. This data forms the foundation for creating segmented and personalized automation sequences that address the specific needs of different customer segments. Behavior-based marketing enables businesses to deliver content and offers that are highly relevant to each individual, ultimately leading to a higher conversion rate and improved customer satisfaction.

To enhance the effectiveness of automation, **it's crucial to align marketing efforts with the customer's journey,** mapping out touchpoints and interactions that correspond to different stages in the buying and decision-making process. By understanding customer behavior at each stage, businesses can design automation sequences that provide timely and relevant communication, guiding prospects towards a purchase with personalized messaging and offers. This approach fosters a sense of understanding and connection, making the customer feel valued and understood throughout their journey.

Behavior-based marketing also enables businesses to identify trigger points, such as specific actions or behaviors that indicate an increased readiness to make a purchase. By recognizing these trigger points, businesses can effectively use automation to deliver targeted content and offers that capitalize on the customer's heightened interest. This not only increases the likelihood of conversion but also enhances the overall customer experience by providing tailored solutions at the right moment.

One of the key benefits of leveraging behavior-based marketing within automation is **the ability to nurture leads and customers in a more personalized and meaningful way.** By understanding the behavior and preferences of the audience, businesses can develop nurturing sequences that cater to individual needs, providing valuable content and guidance that aligns with each person's unique journey. This tailored approach fosters trust and loyalty, positioning the business as a trusted advisor rather than a pushy sales entity.

Finally, **behavior-based marketing amplifies the impact of automation** by enabling businesses to adapt and adjust their messaging in real-time based on customer interactions. By tracking and analyzing customer behavior, businesses can refine their automation sequences, identifying areas for improvement and optimizing the customer experience. This iterative approach ensures that the marketing efforts remain relevant and effective, continuously evolving to meet the changing needs and preferences of the audience.

In essence, behavior-based marketing enhances the effectiveness of automation by allowing businesses to connect with their audience on a deeper level. By leveraging behavioral insights, businesses can create personalized automation sequences that resonate with individuals, leading to increased engagement, customer satisfaction, and ultimately, improved business outcomes.

Embarking on the journey to targeted and impactful marketing starts with personalization at its core. Just like a well-tailored suit impresses at a glance, **personalized automation sequences** captivate, engaging your audience by speaking directly to their specific needs and preferences. It's a powerful strategy, leveraging individual behaviors to create marketing that not only reaches but resonates.

Tailored automation sequences ensure relevance by **triggering**

marketing actions based on user interactions. Imagine the impact of an email that arrives just when a customer is contemplating a repeat purchase or a reminder sent at the exact moment a user re-engages with your app. This is the essence of behavior-based marketing—striking the iron while it's hot to maximize engagement and conversion.

Crafting Personalized Experiences

The mastery of **personalized marketing lies in data**. Every click, purchase, and search is a treasure trove of insight into what your audience values. By utilizing this data, it becomes possible to craft bespoke automation sequences that feel like one-on-one conversations. This approach not only delights customers but also significantly boosts the likelihood of taking the desired action. With a personalized touch, you nudge them gently down the sales funnel, fostering trust and loyalty along the way.

Dynamic Content Tailoring

Dynamic content is a shapeshifter in the world of marketing, modifying itself to the user's profile within your automated emails, websites, and ads. It's a game-changer. By showcasing products that align with past behaviors or suggesting content that mirrors the customer's taste, dynamic content creates an environment of familiarity and ease, almost like a digital concierge that knows what they need before they do.

Real-time personalization goes beyond simple product suggestions; it's about evoking emotions that lead to connections. An abandoned cart email, for example, that not only reminds customers of what they've left behind but also offers tailored advice or a time-sensitive discount, can turn hesitation into action. With relevance as the cornerstone, **personalized automation sequences can create a compelling narrative that guides your customer journey toward a satisfying conclusion**.

Segmentation for Precision

Segmentation slices through the generic to deliver **highly targeted communication**. Separating your audience into detailed segments allows for the creation of nuanced messages that cater to the specific needs and interests of each group. This segmentation can include demographics, buying behavior, engagement levels, and more. By addressing the unique preferences within each segment, your marketing automation becomes a precision tool, carving out paths that are far more likely to result in conversion.

Testing and Learning

Continuous improvement is at the heart of successful behavior-based automation. This requires an ongoing process of **A/B testing**, learning what works and what doesn't, and refining your strategies over time. The key is to test elements like subject lines, images, and calls to action, then analyze the results to understand better what compels your audience to engage. This cycle of testing and improvement ensures your automation sequences remain fresh and effective, keeping pace with the evolving interests of your audience.

Automation Tools at Your Service

There is a myriad of tools available designed to **simplify the creation of personalized automation sequences**. From email marketing platforms to CRM software, these tools come equipped with features like segmentation, behavior tracking, and dynamic content that make it easier to deliver personalized marketing at scale. The key is to choose tools that integrate well with your business processes and provide actionable insights to continually refine your approach.

The transition to behavior-based marketing with personalized automation sequences is a significant step toward achieving a sophisticated and impactful marketing strategy. It's not just selling; it's about building relationships and delivering value at every touchpoint. Implement this strategic shift, and watch your engagement metrics soar, your customer satisfaction enhance, and your brand reputation flourish. Remember, it's a process of constant evolution, where the goal is always to meet your customers exactly where they are with what they need, fostering unshakable loyalty and driving your business to new heights.

In this chapter, we've delved into the power of behavior-based marketing and its ability to supercharge your automation sequences through personalized and targeted strategies. We've learned that understanding the behaviors and preferences of our audience is not just a luxury but a necessity if we want to create impactful marketing efforts.

By tailoring our marketing efforts to meet the specific needs and interests of our audience, we can build a deeper connection and resonance with them. This personalized approach and understanding of their behavior not only enhances the effectiveness of automation but also creates a foundation for stronger, more genuine relationships with our leads and customers.

Personalized automation sequences, driven by behavioral data, enable us to create targeted and impactful marketing strategies that genuinely resonate with our audience. When we can show that we understand and care about their preferences and behaviors, the trust and loyalty we foster will be unmatched.

As we move forward in this book, keep in mind the significance of understanding your audience's behaviors and preferences, as well as the potential of behavior-based marketing to revolutionize your automation sequences. It's not just about efficiency; it's about building a community and scaling your business with heart-centered marketing that truly connects and resonates with your audience.

Chapter 3: Infusing Emotion into Automated Marketing

"To resonate with our customers' hearts, not just their inboxes..."

Outside, the weather churned an ominous brew; a storm was brewing, both in nature and within Elizabeth's chest. Today, Elizabeth had stumbled upon an idea, a glimmer of a solution to the problem that was gnawing at her like a persistent mouse on an old rope. Her company's automated communications seemed cold, robotic, detached from the vibrant, caring heart of the brand she knew they were. How could she inject the warmth of human touch into the pixelated veins of her company's email campaigns?

Seated at her desk, the soft hum of her computer the only accompaniment, her mind wandered to a recent customer feedback report — it was not good. The words "impersonal" and "mechanical" stood out like sore thumbs, reminding her of the distance between their automated messages and the core of what they once promised. "To resonate with our customers' hearts, not just their inboxes..." she whispered, recalling part of their old mission statement.

Her fingers curled around a warm mug of coffee, the aroma embracing her senses and offering a fleeting comfort, much like the good old days when customer relationships were as rich and warm as the beverage in her hands. Suddenly, a thought: Could empathy be coded? She pondered the intricacies of emotional intelligence and wondered if the digital realm had room for authenticity and the heartfelt connect that many brands seemed to have neglected.

Elizabeth recalled a time when she received a message so finely tuned to her emotions it felt like it had been written just for her. It had brought a tear to her eye, and right there, she knew there was power, immense power, in emotional resonance. "That's it," she thought. "We need our customers to feel understood, to feel that behind every byte is a beating heart."

She began to draft her proposal, envisioning automated communications that spoke to fears, celebrated victories, and acknowledged the consumer's journey with a relatable human touch. Each word on her screen was chosen with care, aiming to influence, to provide a beacon of connection in the digital abyss. She knew in her heart that authentic connections would not only guide customer decisions but also foster those all-important meaningful relationships.

Yet, as the clouds outside billowed and crashed, a sliver of doubt sliced through Elizabeth's resolve. Can algorithms ever truly embody the nuances of human empathy? It was a question she knew she had to answer, for her customers and for the integrity of her brand. Could this be the turning point she had been seeking, not just for company revenue, but for redefining value in a world that was becoming increasingly automated? How can one ensure that in the pursuit of efficiency, the essence of human connection isn't lost?

Unleash the Power of Emotions in Your Automated Messages

Automated marketing doesn't mean your business should lose its heartbeat. The key to amplifying your impact lies in the delicate art of **infusing emotion into every automated interaction**. As digital networks expand and technology grows more sophisticated, **it's crucial not to forget the human touch**—the genuine connection between brand and customer that transcends mere transaction. This call for authenticity is echoed in the choices of today's consumers, who increasingly rally around brands that embody values and emotions they resonate with. Embracing the strategic use of **emotional intelligence within automated systems** can differentiate your business in the crowded digital bazaar and root a sense of loyalty within your community.

Infusing emotion into automated communications is no mere whimsy; it's a potent strategy for **building stronger, more sustainable**

customer relationships. Whether we recognize it or not, emotions heavily influence purchasing behaviors. When businesses understand and use this to their advantage, automations become not just a tool for scalability but also a platform for **meaningful connection**. Integrating such a philosophy requires forethought. It demands we redefine the boundaries of automation, striding beyond efficiency and stepping squarely into the realm of **empathy, authenticity, and relatability**.

To truly resonate with your audience and drive decision-making, automated marketing should mirror the nuances of human communication. This chapter is your guide to achieving that resonance. Dive into the **psychology of emotional engagement** and learn to weave it seamlessly into your communications fabric. Deconstruct the walls between man and machine, and discover the secrets to crafting automated messages that sound less like robotic monologues and more like a **conversation with a trusted confidante**.

With practical advice rooted in the latest marketing insights, implementing these emotional drivers into your automated efforts is not just theory but a reality you can achieve today. By the end of this chapter, you will possess actionable strategies to blend the efficiency of automation with the warmth and relatability of personal interaction. Gone are the days when automated messages felt impersonal; welcome to an era where every automated touchpoint can **exude heart and drive home impact**, fostering deeper bonds with those who matter most to your business.

Emotional Intelligence: Your Marketing Automation's Missing Ingredient

It's time to harness the full **spectrum of human emotion** to engage and retain your customers. Understand the *impact of evoking emotions* in automated communications and transform your marketing into a vibrant tapestry that tugs at the heartstrings as it seamlessly guides consumers. Journey into the core of motivational cues and emerge with the *key to unlock binding emotional convictions* within your automated messages.

The distance between indifferent scrolling and a captivated audience lies in the **sincerity of your story**. Learn to infuse authenticity into every automated message, crafting a narrative that isn't simply broadcasted but felt. Authenticity is not a buzzword but a fundament upon which strong brands are built. When your automation echoes **true empathy**, your community will not only listen; they will engage, advocate, and remain.

Crafting Connections that Count

Create deeper connections through automation by inserting the essence of human interaction—**relatability**. Envision your automated systems as bridges, not barriers, to rich, ongoing dialogues with your audience. By honing in on shared experiences and commonalities, your brand becomes a living entity with which customers can relate on a personal level. Relationship-building isn't about broadcasting—it's about conversing, understanding, and growing together.

Discover how **emotional resonance not only complements but amplifies your marketing automation**. As you weave these principles into your communications, you'll observe a shift: customers transition from passively receiving messages to actively seeking engagement with your brand. Witness this transformative approach in action; stories from within the industry serve as your roadmap, illustrating the tangible success achieved through empathetic, automated outreach.

It's time to evoke, connect, and engage on a whole new level. Leverage the full potential of your automated marketing, and sculpt an empire that thrives on **emotional equity**. Your automated systems are ready to be the conduit for the passionate pulse of your brand. Welcome to the future of marketing—**automated, yet deeply human**.

Automated marketing has become an essential tool for businesses looking to scale their operations while maintaining a personal connection with their audience. However, the true impact of automated communications on building stronger customer relationships goes beyond just efficiency and convenience. In fact, evoking emotion in automated marketing holds the key to fostering deeper connections with your audience. This emotional resonance influences customer decisions and nurtures meaningful relationships that can drive long-term success for your business.

Why Emotion Matters

Emotion is a powerful force in human interactions, and it's no different in the realm of marketing. When you infuse your automated communications with authenticity, empathy, and relatability, you create a deeper connection with your audience. This connection goes beyond the transactional, sparking emotions and building a rapport that can lead to long-term loyalty and advocacy.

The Impact of Evoking Emotion

Emotion has a profound impact on decision-making. When your automated messages strike an emotional chord with your audience, they are more likely to engage, respond, and ultimately convert. For example, a well-crafted automated email that speaks to the pain points and aspirations of your audience can elicit a strong emotional response, leading to higher open and click-through rates, and ultimately, more conversions.

Building Stronger Customer Relationships

By infusing emotion into your automated communications, you're not just driving sales; you're also building stronger, more meaningful relationships with your customers. When customers feel understood, valued, and supported, they are more likely to remain loyal and become brand advocates. This loyalty can be invaluable to the long-term success of your business, as it leads to repeat purchases and referrals, fueling growth and sustainability.

Embracing Emotion in Automation

Understanding the impact of evoking emotion in automated communications is the first step in harnessing the power of emotional resonance. From crafting compelling copy that speaks directly to your audience's emotions to personalizing automated messages to resonate with individual experiences, embracing emotion in automation is crucial for fostering genuine connections with your audience.

Moving Forward with Purpose

As you continue your journey through the chapters of this book, you'll discover practical strategies and actionable insights for infusing authenticity, empathy, and relatability into your automated marketing efforts. You'll also explore how this emotional resonance influences customer decisions and fosters meaningful, long-lasting relationships that can fuel the growth and success of your business. So, let's dive into the next part and unlock the secrets of infusing authenticity and empathy into your automated communications.

In the next section, you'll learn to craft compelling, emotionally resonant automated messages that connect with your audience on a deeper level.

Building strong customer relationships through automated marketing requires the infusion of authenticity, empathy, and relatability into your communications. When you infuse your automated messages with these qualities, you create a deeper connection with your audience, which has a profound impact on their decision-making process and loyalty to your brand.

Authenticity is the foundation of any successful relationship, and it's no different in marketing. When your audience feels that your messages are genuine and sincere, they are more likely to engage with your brand. Authenticity in automation means delivering messages that reflect your brand's true voice and values. It involves being transparent, honest, and consistent in your communication, which will foster trust and credibility with your audience.

Empathy is the ability to understand and share the feelings of your audience. Infusing empathy into your automated marketing involves showing genuine concern for your customers' needs and challenges. It means addressing their pain points and providing solutions in a compassionate and understanding manner. By demonstrating empathy in your automated messages, you create a sense of connection and emotional resonance with your audience that goes beyond transactional interactions.

Relatability is about creating messages that your audience can connect with on a personal level. It involves understanding your audience's experiences, preferences, and lifestyles to tailor your messages accordingly. When your audience feels that your brand understands them and speaks their language, they are more likely to feel a sense of belonging and loyalty. This relatability can be achieved through personalized content, storytelling, and showcasing real customer experiences.

To infuse authenticity, empathy, and relatability into your automated marketing, start by **developing a clear understanding of your audience**. This involves conducting thorough market research, analyzing customer data, and creating detailed buyer personas. By knowing who your audience is, what they care about, and what challenges they face, you can tailor your automated messages to resonate with their needs and emotions.

Next, **craft your messaging with genuine care and consideration**. Be thoughtful about the language, tone, and imagery you use in your automated communications. Ensure that your messages reflect your brand's values and evoke the emotions you want your audience to feel. Avoid generic, one-size-fits-all messages and instead, strive to create content that feels personal and relevant to each recipient.

Another critical step is to **leverage personalization and segmentation** to deliver messages that are tailored to your audience's specific interests and preferences. Use customer data to personalize your automated messages, such as addressing recipients by their names, recommending products based on their purchase history, and providing content that aligns with their interests.

Additionally, **incorporate storytelling into your automated**

communications to create an emotional connection with your audience. Share compelling narratives that resonate with your audience's experiences and emotions, allowing them to see themselves in the stories you tell. This approach humanizes your brand and makes your messaging more relatable and engaging.

Remember that infusing authenticity, empathy, and relatability into your automated marketing strategy is an ongoing process that requires **continuous evaluation and refinement**. Regularly monitor the performance of your automated messages, gather feedback from your audience, and adjust your approach based on the insights you gain. By constantly evolving your communication strategy, you can ensure that your messages remain impactful and meaningful to your audience.

The Power of Emotional Resonance in Customer Decisions

The heart of compelling automated marketing isn't simply in the data crunching or strategic timing; **it's the emotional resonance** that a message carries, pivotal in guiding customer decisions. Remarkably, behavioral scientists have uncovered that emotions create distinctive patterns in the brain, which in turn shape the decisions consumers make. Recognizing this dynamic, savvy marketers are harnessing the power of emotional resonance, using it as a catalyst within automated marketing streams to elevate their strategies from informative to influential.

Crafting Authenticity in Automated Messages

Creating authenticity in automated communications is no mere buzzword; it's a strategic move to captivate your audience. Authentic marketing speaks with a *voice of honesty*, forges a bond, and establishes trust with your customers. This is critical because when customers feel that a brand's message aligns with their values and experiences, their trust deepens, and their loyalty solidifies. The trick lies in maintaining a consistent tone that reflects your brand's core values and message across all automated platforms, from email campaigns to social media posts.

Empathy: The Bridge to Customer Loyalty

Integrating empathy into automated marketing is akin to personalizing a well-crafted gift: it shows you understand and care for your customers. Demonstrating empathy means recognizing emotions and responding appropriately—through targeted content that addresses current customer concerns or joys. It means acknowledging your customer's journey, recognizing their pain points, and offering solutions before they even ask. By doing so, you are not just selling a product or service; **you are providing a helping hand**, which can be a powerful motivator in a customer's decision to stay loyal to your brand.

Relatable Content Wins Hearts

Relatability in marketing is all about finding common ground with your audience. Use segments of information about your customer demographics to tailor messages that resonate with their everyday lives. By doing this, automated marketing can feel personal and relevant, transforming a generic message into one that appears handpicked for the individual. Relatable content is also inherently shareable, as people are often moved to share experiences that resonate with them on a personal level. Encouraging this kind of interaction not only spreads the message further but also reinforces the bond between brand and customer.

Measuring Success Through Emotional Engagement

Tracking the success of emotional resonance in marketing is as important as the strategy itself. Analyzing customer engagement, through metrics such as click-through rates, time spent on content, or direct feedback, provides insight into how well your emotional messaging connects with the audience. Additionally, keep an eye on customer retention rates and repeat purchases, as these are strong indicators of the emotional bond customers feel with your brand. With these metrics, you can refine your approach, discovering what truly strikes a chord with your audience and leading to sustained emotional engagement.

Stories That Stick: Using Narrative to Engage

Storytelling in automated marketing isn't just about presenting a sequence of events; it's about crafting narratives that *stick* with your audience long after they've been told. Sharing success stories or testimonials from satisfied customers imbue your automated messages with a human element. Stories lead to identification and empathy, fostering a sense of community among your audience. They illustrate not just the functionality of a service or product but its impact on real lives, making it relatable and desirable.

Continuous Improvement: The Cycle of Emotional Optimization

Emotional resonance isn't a set-it-and-forget-it aspect of marketing; it requires ongoing adjustments and a keen sensitivity to customer feedback. Just as personal relationships grow and evolve, so too must your approach to automated marketing. Regularly revisiting and fine-tuning your automated communications ensures they stay fresh, relevant, and emotionally appealing. Engage in A/B testing to compare different emotional approaches, collect data, and optimize accordingly. This iterative process underlines a commitment to nurturing customer relationships genuinely and effectively.

Leveraging Automation to Build Enduring Bonds

In a digital landscape that can often feel impersonal, strategically infusing emotional resonance into automated marketing can be transformative, engendering profound connections between brand and customer. **These connections are the lifelines of businesses—far-reaching and enduring.** As you deploy automation to its full potential, let the human touch be the guide, ensuring every message strengthens the relationship, resonates emotionally, and, above all, feels genuinely personal to each recipient. With the insights provided here, your automated campaigns will not only capture attention but hold hearts, paving the way for a thriving, emotionally engaged community around your brand.

In the fast-paced world of automated marketing, the ability to connect with your audience on an emotional level is a game-changer. By infusing authenticity, empathy, and relatability into your automated communications, you can create a deeper, more meaningful connection with your audience. This, in turn, influences their decision-making process and fosters stronger, more loyal relationships with your brand.

Understanding the impact of evoking emotion in automated communications is a crucial step toward building stronger customer relationships. Emotions play a powerful role in shaping customer behavior, and by tapping into these emotions, you can create a more compelling and resonant marketing message.

As you move forward in implementing emotion-infused marketing

automation, remember to keep the following in mind:

- **Authenticity:** Stay true to your brand's voice and values, and always strive to communicate in a genuine and relatable manner.
- **Empathy:** Put yourself in your customers' shoes and address their pain points and needs with compassion and understanding.
- **Relatability:** Share stories and experiences that your audience can connect with, creating a sense of familiarity and trust.

The emotional resonance you create through your automated marketing efforts will directly influence customer decisions. By tailoring your messages to evoke the right emotions, you can inspire action and create lasting connections with your audience.

In the next chapter, we'll explore how to leverage these emotional connections to drive meaningful engagement and ultimately, build a massive community that is deeply connected to your brand.

Chapter 4: Designing the Client Journey for Nurturing Automation

"Let the machine handle the mundane so you can captain the extraordinary."

In the bustling heart of the city, where skyscrapers sliced the sky and humanity's fervent hustle was as natural as breathing, Lydia stood before the behemoth of glass and steel, her sanctuary and battlefield – the marketing agency she called her forge. Thoughts raced as she navigated the cacophony of the lobby, the click of her heels on marble a steady metronome amidst the symphony of chatter and commerce. The elevators shuttled their inhabitants, indifferent to the burden of ambition they bore upward.

Today's challenge was not in design nor in pitch but in breathing life into the abstract – the journey of the client, a path she had traversed many times yet struggled to map. Lydia pondered the ebb and flow of relationships cultivated discreetly through digits and displays, each touchpoint automated yet yearning to feel as though woven by human hands. Nurturing, she realized, was more than a sequence of well-timed emails and cleverly crafted messages; it was the invisible thread stitching the client to the brand, an inaudible whisper of trust and anticipation.

Amidst the hiss of the espresso machine and the low hum of the air conditioners, Lydia found a moment of serenity in her office, the setting sun painting the horizon with strokes of orange and lavender. Her gaze lingered on the cityscape, a grid of potentialities, each intersection a meeting, every avenue a lead. And yet the crux lay in weaving automation with sincerity, a paradox she reveled in unraveling.

She recalled the words of a mentor, spoken years ago but echoing afresh, "Eighty percent automation, Lydia. Let the machine handle the mundane so you can captain the extraordinary." Her mind composed a symphony of if-then scenarios, each chord a trigger, every measure a step in the dance between company and client. She envisioned a conduit that ferried her leads from the first hello to the warmth of gratitude that would inevitably birth referral – the highest accolade.

How could she orchestrate a client's journey, synchronizing each note, from lead acquisition to that final crowning moment of referral? How to inlay the entire route with a comforting presence, the soft assurance that in every digital whisper, there was a steady, nurturing heart beating?

As the day waned and the office breathed its last corporate sigh, Lydia lingered, a solitary figure against the dwindling light. A vision began to crystallize, a blueprint of engagement and care, a strategy not yet fully formed but yearning to be birthed.

Can the artistry of human connection truly be encoded into the binary world of automation?

From First Click to Lasting Loyalty: Mastering the Automated Client Odyssey

In the realm of automated marketing, the journey we craft for our clients is much like a well-oiled machine, ideally running with precision yet brimming with the warmth of human touch. Embracing the concept that nurturing is not merely a transaction but a fundamental part of the relationship-building process, we embark on a quest to design a client journey that is both nurturing and efficiently automated. Evoking a seamless experience from initial interest to the ultimate act of referral, our strategy is to keep the essence of community and connection at the forefront of automated marketing, proving that technology and compassion are not mutually exclusive.

The exponent of success lies in the careful orchestration of every interaction, nurturing clients through a tailored path that feels personal, even in its automation. As thought leaders in the burgeoning empire of automated marketing, we must wield these powerful tools with intent, ensuring that each automated touchpoint aligns with the delicate human needs of our audience. This chapter is the blueprint to that empire, where automation meets personalization, ensuring that clients feel supported at every twist and turn on their journey.

Grasping the importance of the client journey is the inception point. It begins with a meticulous plan that understands the nuances of each phase a client encounters. **To nurture is to recognize the stages of the customer lifecycle** and to leverage automated interventions that resonate with the client's evolving requirements. By doing so, we set the stage for a narrative that delivers consistency without compromise, ensuring no lead is left unattended and no opportunity for connection is missed.

As we delve deeply into the chapters of this grand design, learning to create a seamless flow from lead acquisition to customer satisfaction is paramount. It's not merely about ushering clients through a funnel; it's about **enriching the passage with moments of genuine care and insight**. Here, nurturing automation translates into a sphere where every automated email, every scheduled post, and every trigger-based message serves to affirm the client's significance in the vast community we aim to cultivate.

Discovering strategies for a nurturing and supportive client journey also involves recognizing the delicate balance between efficiency and personalization. **The art lies in striking a chord with the** client—understanding the underlying rhythm of their preferences and behaviors, and responding with automation that feels anything but automatic. This is the harmony we aim to achieve: potent, responsive automation that reverberates with the individual's tempo and timbre.

Crafting a Symphony of Emails: The Automated Yet Personal Touch

The Anatomy of an Email Campaign: Crafting Messages that Motivate and Move

Step 1: **Define Your Goals**

Before diving into the depths of email marketing, set your compass by defining clear, measurable goals. Determine what success looks like—be it boosting sales, increasing event attendance, or enhancing brand awareness. Understanding the destination ensures every crafted message propels you closer to your aspirations.

Step 2: **Identify Your Target Audience**

Knowledge of your audience is your greatest asset. Pinpoint their desires, obstacles, and what sets their hearts racing. Armed with this insight, mold your content to strike a chord that resonates through their core.

Step 3: **Craft Compelling Subject Lines**

The subject line is your first handshake—make it firm and memorable. Be concise and intriguing, sparking curiosity with a personal touch. Here, you're the tastemaker, setting the tone for the rich content that lies within.

Step 4: **Create Engaging Content**

Content is king and context its kingdom. Cultivate value in every word, ensuring relevance and readability. Speak as if in quiet conversation with the reader, inviting them to journey further with a clear, compelling call to action.

Step 5: **Design Attention-Grabbing Templates**

Visuals carve the path to engagement, serving as mile-markers for your narrative. Let your template mirror your ethos, simple yet stimulating. Responsive design is your ally—beyond the desktop lies a mobile frontier.

Step 6: **Set Up Automation and Email Sequences**

Automation is your silent envoy, delivering messages with precision and grace. Tailor sequences to the individual, adjusting to the ebb and flow of their engagement. Forge connections with content that reflects their journey.

Step 7: **Test, Analyze, and Optimize**

The cycle of improvement is perpetual. Test assumptions, refine techniques, and polish your prose. Your audience's response is the crucible in which your campaign is refined and your tactics are honed for the ultimate resonance.

Step 8: **Monitor and Measure Results**

Metrics are the lens through which we perceive success. Monitor diligently, measure wisely, interpret judiciously. Within these numbers lies the map to improved engagement, sharpening your aim for the next venture.

By adhering to these steps, we launch not just a campaign but a vessel for connection. Join us as we chart the course for a community bonded not by transactions, but by shared experiences, nurtured through the mastery of the automated client journey.

Creating a seamless client journey and automating key touchpoints is at the heart of nurturing automation. When every step from lead acquisition to satisfied customer referral is carefully designed and efficiently automated, it ensures a consistent and supportive experience for your audience at every stage. Defining the client journey and automating at least 80 percent of it is crucial for nurturing automation.

Defining the Client Journey

The client journey is the path that a potential customer takes from the moment they discover your brand to the moment they become a loyal customer and advocate. Every touchpoint along this journey, from the initial interaction to the final sale, plays a critical role in shaping the customer's experience and perception of your brand. Understanding and defining this journey is essential for creating a personalized and nurturing experience for your audience at every stage.

Automating Key Touchpoints for Efficiency

Automation is the key to ensuring that no client falls through the cracks and that every interaction is carefully designed to nurture and support your audience. By automating key touchpoints, such as lead nurturing, onboarding, and post-purchase follow-up, you can create a seamless and efficient experience for your clients while saving time and resources.

Designing a client journey that is consistently nurturing and supportive at every stage, and automating key touchpoints, is the foundation for building a loyal community of engaged customers. When every step is thoughtfully designed for nurturing and support, it ensures that your audience feels valued and guided throughout their journey with your brand.

Read on to learn how to create a seamless flow from

lead acquisition to satisfied customer referral through automation.

Creating a seamless flow from lead acquisition to satisfied customer referral through automation is a critical aspect of nurturing and expanding a business. By optimizing and automating every touchpoint along the client journey, you can foster consistent and efficient nurturing, leading to satisfied customers who are eager to refer others to your business. This process goes beyond automation; it requires a thoughtful design that focuses on guiding leads from initial contact to becoming loyal customers. To achieve this, it's essential to understand the journey your client will take, from the first interaction to becoming a brand advocate, and to streamline and automate key touchpoints to ensure a nurturing and supportive experience at every stage.

Start by mapping out the entire client journey, from the moment they first encounter your brand to their eventual referral of others. This bird's-eye view allows you to anticipate and plan for every interaction and touchpoint along the way. **Identify the pivotal stages of the journey, such as initial contact, purchase, post-purchase support, and advocacy, ensuring that each is optimized for efficient and nurturing automation.** A clear understanding of this journey gives you the insight needed to design a seamless flow that is both effective and nurturing at every step.

Next, focus on creating a streamlined process that guides leads through each stage of the client journey. **Automate the delivery of valuable content, personalized messages, and seamless transactions, ensuring a smooth and engaging experience for your audience.** By harnessing the power of automation, you can remove friction points and provide a consistent and nurturing experience, no matter where each lead is in the journey.

Utilize automation tools and platforms to design workflows that cater to each stage of the client journey. **Leverage customer relationship management (CRM) systems, email marketing platforms, and marketing automation tools to orchestrate a seamless and personalized experience for leads.** These tools allow you to automate the delivery of targeted content, track customer interactions, and personalize communications, ensuring that each lead receives the nurturing support they need to progress through the journey.

Incorporate feedback loops into your automated processes to continuously optimize and refine the client journey. **Gather data on customer interactions, engagement, and feedback, and use this information to fine-tune your automation strategies.** By analyzing the data, you can identify areas for improvement, refine your nurturing processes, and ensure that every touchpoint is optimized for maximum impact.

Finally, aim to create a client journey that not only converts leads into customers but also nurtures them into satisfied advocates for your brand. **Craft an automation strategy that focuses on delivering**

exceptional customer experiences, providing top-notch support, and incentivizing referrals. By nurturing customers beyond the initial sale, you can turn them into enthusiastic advocates who are eager to share their positive experiences with others, fueling the growth of your business through word-of-mouth referrals.

Designing a client journey that is both nurturing and supportive requires a strategic approach to ensure consistency at every stage. This begins by mapping out the entire client experience from the initial contact to the final stage of customer advocacy. Automation plays a pivotal role in this process but must be paired with a deep understanding of the client's needs, preferences, and behaviors. Each interaction must leave the client feeling valued and understood, affirming that they have made the right choice in entrusting their needs to your business.

Personalization at Scale

Ironically, automation, seen by some as impersonal, is exactly what enables personalization at scale. Utilize automation to segment your audience based on their interactions, behaviors, and purchases. This allows for **targeted communication** that speaks directly to their needs. For example, if a customer has shown interest in a particular service, automation can schedule follow-up emails discussing this service in more detail, perhaps offering a case study or customer testimony that resonates with their segment. Implement dynamic content in emails that changes according to each recipient's profile, serving them bespoke messages that foster a unique connection.

Seamless Integration

A client journey devoid of friction is the cornerstone of nurturing automation. Ensure that all systems — from CRM (Customer Relationship Management) software to email marketing platforms and sales funnels — are seamlessly integrated. This eliminates data silos and provides a unified view of the client's journey, *empowering you to respond proactively* to their needs. For instance, should a lead download a resource from your site, an integrated system can immediately trigger a series of educational emails that nurtures this potential client through the sales pipeline.

Nurturing Feedback Loops

Incorporate mechanisms for feedback collection at various stages of the client journey. Listening to your clients and acting on their feedback is a critical nurturing strategy. Automation can send out surveys after product usage or service completion to gauge satisfaction and collect valuable insights. These insights can then inform product development, customer service training, and marketing messaging, ensuring continuous improvement and client-centric evolution of your services.

Value-Driven Content Distribution

Content is the lifeblood of client nurturing. Utilize automation to distribute value-driven content regularly. By analyzing user interactions with previous content, automate the delivery of articles, videos, or webinars that address their specific interests and needs. Content that solves problems or adds value enhances trust and reinforces your status as an authority in your field. It is essential to create a content calendar that aligns with various stages of the client journey and reliably delivers this content via automated systems.

Consistency and Timeliness

The timing of your engagements can significantly impact how nurturing they feel to the client. Automate the delivery of messages to ensure they are sent at the optimal time for engagement. For instance, sending a check-in email after a client has received a product to ensure everything is satisfactory, or a birthday discount, can leave a lasting positive impression. *Consistent nurturing* builds trust and creates a client experience that feels personalized and attentive.

Predictive Analytics for Proactivity

Harness the power of predictive analytics to anticipate client needs before they fully materialize. By analyzing data, AI algorithms can predict when a client may need a service upgrade or when they might be at risk for churn. Automation tools can be set up to act upon these predictions, reaching out with relevant offers or support to turn potential issues into opportunities for re-engagement and continual nurturing.

Training and Empowering Teams

Even the best automation is only as effective as the team behind it. Train your team to understand and manage nurturing automation tools effectively. This empowers them to make real-time decisions to enhance the client experience. For example, a sales team that has access to real-time behavioral data can personalize their sales approach, while support staff equipped with a client's history can resolve issues more efficiently and considerately.

In essence, every interaction in the client journey should feel like a step forward in a mutually beneficial relationship. By automating nurturing strategies, you can ensure that the consistency, personalization, and attentiveness that build long-lasting client relationships are maintained at scale. This not only optimizes the client experience but also frees up valuable time for your team to focus on high-level strategy and personal interactions that require a human touch. Keep the human aspect alive in your business, and let automation bolster your efforts to make every client journey a testament to your commitment to quality, care, and innovation.

In this chapter, we've delved into the crucial role of defining the client journey and automating key touchpoints for efficient nurturing. We've explored the significance of creating a seamless flow from lead acquisition to satisfied customer referral through automation. Moreover, we've uncovered strategies for designing a client journey that is consistently nurturing and supportive at every stage.

Now, it's time to take action and apply these principles to your own business. **Start by mapping out your client journey** from the first point of contact to post-purchase follow-up. Identify the key touchpoints where automation can enhance the nurturing process, allowing you to focus on building deeper connections with your audience.

Next, implement automation tools that streamline and optimize each touchpoint. Look for platforms that offer personalized messaging, segmentation, and scheduling capabilities to ensure that your nurturing efforts are tailored to each individual in your audience.

Lastly, monitor and analyze the results of your nurturing automation. Use key performance indicators to measure the effectiveness of your automated touchpoints and make adjustments as needed to continuously improve the client journey.

By grasping the importance of defining the client journey and automating key touchpoints, you've taken a significant step toward building a nurturing and supportive experience for your audience. With the right strategy in place, you can create a client journey that not only drives conversions but also builds lasting relationships with your customers.

Chapter 5: Long-Term Nurture Sequences for Sustained Engagement

"Transcending the Transaction: Nurturing Lasts a Lifetime"

The coffee shop buzzed with the quiet hum of life as people dotted the small tables, pretending to immerse themselves in their laptops and smartphones. Among them sat Valerie, sipping slowly from a cup that had long ago given up the warmth of its contents. Her gaze alternated between the busy barista, who was like a conductor guiding an orchestra of coffee machines, and the slowly blinking cursor on her own laptop screen. It was a peculiar dance of procrastination.

Valerie's mission was clear, or at least that's what she had led herself to believe when she accepted the role of Marketing Director at a startup that prided itself on disrupting the traditional e-commerce landscape. Yet she found herself wrestling with something more profound than just another promotional campaign — the art of mastering long-term customer relationships. Her mind circled the concept of nurture sequences, an approach she glimpsed as capable of fostering loyalty and trust, yet daunting in her uncertainty of its execution.

She was well aware that the quick-fire tactics of her past successes, those transactional emails that converted so well, played a limited part in this new chapter. As Valerie pondered, the flavor of her coffee seemed to manifest as a metaphor in her mind — a quick burst of caffeine that spiked one's attention but left one craving for more, soon after. She needed something richer, a blend that would keep customers coming back because they felt seen and understood over time.

The patter of a raindrop gently rapped on the window beside her, drawing her attention momentarily to the gloom outside. Congruent with her thoughts, she realized that her relationship with customers couldn't be as transient as the weather, it needed a continuity akin to the perennial oaks lining the street, which stood strong regardless of the storm. Her laptop chimed with a new email — a customer's positive feedback. Her lips curved subtly into a smile, a rare moment of resolve cutting through the ambiguity.

With renewed vigor, Valerie started to outline her strategy, cognizant of the fact that this was not about simply selling a product once. It was about inviting someone into a narrative, her company's narrative, one where the customer was as much a character as the brand itself. Implementing the nurture sequences meant that every email, blog post, and social media update needed to carry the integrity of a brand that appreciated the customer beyond the 'Thank You for Your Purchase' page.

Would her visualization of a community, fostered through thoughtful, continuous engagement, come to fruition? Would these customers, feeling valued and considered, become the brand evangelists she sought to cultivate? Such were the questions lingering in Valerie's heart as her fingers moved rhythmically across the keyboard, translating these intentions into actions.

As the evening crept in and the coffee shop's lights grew bolder against the approaching night, Valerie packed away her aspirations with her laptop. The rain had eased, replaced by the subtle song of evening traffic. Perhaps, as she walked home through the crisp air, the true measure of her strategy's success lay not just in metrics, but in the real human connections that it might foster. After all, isn't that what every person seeks — to be nurtured and to belong? Could this be the essence of business loyalty, and had she just unlocked the first door to it with her strategy?

Transcending the Transaction: Nurturing Lasts a Lifetime

In the age of instant gratification, it's tempting to chase the quick wins and short-term spikes in sales. But savvy marketers and business leaders understand that the true gold lies in fostering enduring relationships with customers. Automated engagement shouldn't be a fleeting courtship; it's about commitment and nurturing a growing connection. **Long-term nurture sequences** stand at the heart of maintaining customer loyalty and compelling engagement, transforming your automated systems from robotic to heartfelt.

Relationships, as life teaches us, are not built overnight. The same principle applies with unrivaled clarity to customer relationships. It's time to embrace the power of nurture sequences as a strategic imperative for businesses. Step into a world where every email, every message, and every interaction is an investment in your customer's trust and your business's future. Here, you learn to **foster rapport and credibility**, not through forceful sales tactics, but through authentic, value-driven communication.

Imagine a scenario where customers don't just make a purchase; they embark on a journey with your brand, a journey they trust and value. By mastering nurture sequences, you can steer this journey with finesse, guiding them from initial curiosity to loyal advocacy. You'll draw customers closer, not through sheer persistence, but by showing up with genuine intent and helpful solutions. In these chapters, we unfold the blueprint for constructing systems that affirm your customers' choices to engage with your brand for the long haul.

We often misconceive automation as cold and impersonal, but when wielded with care, it can be the most attentive partner in maintaining customer dialogue. *How can we make our machines more human?* By embedding our warmest communication skills into automated sequences. These systems are then forged to check in regularly, provide valuable insights, and express gratitude, developing a dialogue indistinguishable from one-on-one interactions.

Harnessing these strategies isn't just about nurturing leads; it's about nurturing a community. It sets the stage for customers to turn into brand ambassadors, extolling your virtues far and wide. Implementing long-term nurture sequences becomes a testament to your dedication not just to sell, but to serve your audience. This chapter will show you the fundamental steps to create a nurturing environment that keeps your audience engaged, appreciated, and ready to speak volumes about your brand's impact on their lives.

The evidence is clear: relationships nurtured over time yield remarkable dividends. Dive deep into this reservoir of relationship-building strategy, and emerge with a robust set of tools designed to keep your audience engaged, inspired, and loyal. **Expect to discover a profound shift in focus**, from fleeting transactions to enduring relationships, from short-lived contacts to lifelong customers. This is not just an upgrade to your marketing arsenal; it's a transformation of how you do business.

Embrace this narrative with an open heart and expect your customers to reciprocate. With every action guided by the nurturing philosophy, your business sets a new bar for what it means to truly engage. Embark on this imperative journey through the subsequent sections and arm yourself with techniques that will ensure your community not only grows but thrives. The path ahead is illuminated with the promise of sustained relationships and *engagement that resonates with the very core of your customers' values and needs.* Let's stride forward, shaping an empire built on the time-tested foundations of trust and genuine connection.

Long-term nurture sequences are the backbone of sustained customer engagement and loyalty. While quick conversions may result in immediate sales, it's the long-term relationships and trust built through continuous nurture sequences that lay the foundation for lasting customer loyalty. By focusing on nurturing automation that extends beyond just transactional conversions, businesses can have a more profound impact on their customers and build a loyal community.

Long-term nurture sequences allow businesses to connect with their audience on a deeper level, addressing their evolving needs and providing ongoing value. This sustained engagement fosters a sense of trust and reliability, ultimately leading to a more loyal customer base. In a digital world where competition is fierce and attention spans are fleeting, nurturing relationships over time is what sets successful businesses apart.

Moreover, long-term nurture sequences enable businesses to provide personalized and targeted communication, catering to the unique preferences and behaviors of individual customers. By delivering relevant content that resonates with their audience, businesses can create a more meaningful connection, leading to sustained engagement and ultimately, higher customer retention rates.

In contrast to the limited scope of immediate conversions, long-term nurture sequences allow businesses to guide their audience through a journey of evolution and growth. It's not just about closing a deal; it's about nurturing relationships, understanding the needs of customers, and ultimately growing together with them. This approach builds a strong foundation for sustainable business growth and long-term success.

Implementing long-term nurture sequences is an investment in the future of a business. Rather than focusing solely on short-term gains, businesses that prioritize building enduring relationships through nurturing automation are positioning themselves for continued success. The sustained engagement and loyalty fostered through long-term nurture sequences are invaluable assets that contribute to the longevity and prosperity of a business.

By understanding the significance of long-term nurture sequences, businesses can empower themselves with the knowledge and insight needed to build a loyal and engaged customer community. Through continuous nurturing and relationship-building, businesses establish themselves as more than just a service provider, becoming a trusted partner in the journey of their customers' growth and success.

Now, let's explore the benefits of focusing on building relationships and trust over time through nurture sequences.

Building relationships and trust over time through long-term nurture sequences is not just a nice-to-have, it's an essential strategy for sustained customer loyalty and engagement. By focusing on nurturing relationships rather than solely seeking immediate conversions, businesses can unlock a myriad of benefits. **Here are some of the key advantages of prioritizing long-term nurture sequences:**

Firstly, establishing a **consistent and trust-based relationship** with customers over time cultivates a sense of loyalty. When customers feel seen, heard, and understood, they are more likely to remain engaged and loyal to a brand. This loyalty translates into **repeat purchases, referrals, and advocacy**, ultimately contributing to the business's long-term success.

Fostering relationships through long-term nurture sequences also provides an opportunity to **deepen customer understanding**. By maintaining ongoing communication and observing customer interactions, businesses can gain valuable insights into their needs, preferences, and pain points. These insights can then be used to tailor products, services, and marketing efforts to better meet customer expectations.

Another significant benefit is the ability to **nurture customer satisfaction and retention**. Consistent and thoughtful engagement through long-term nurture sequences can greatly contribute to customer satisfaction by addressing their needs and concerns. As a result, customers are more likely to remain subscribed, renew their memberships, and continue engaging with the brand.

In addition, focusing on long-term nurture sequences **reduces the reliance on transactional relationships**. Instead of solely focusing on immediate conversions, businesses that prioritize long-term nurturing build a more sustainable and resilient customer base. This approach shifts the focus from short-term gains to the rewarding and enduring process of building lasting, meaningful connections with customers.

Furthermore, investing in long-term nurture sequences lays the foundation for **long-term brand evangelism**. As customers feel appreciated and valued through ongoing engagement, they are more likely to become advocates for the brand. They may share their positive experiences with others, leading to organic growth and increased brand visibility.

By prioritizing long-term nurture sequences, businesses also demonstrate their commitment to a **customer-centric approach**. This approach emphasizes the importance of understanding and meeting the unique needs of individual customers. This not only contributes to higher customer satisfaction but also sets the stage for meaningful, long-term relationships.

In summary, the benefits of focusing on building relationships and trust over time through long-term nurture sequences are vast and far-reaching. From fostering loyalty and advocacy to deepening understanding and satisfaction, these benefits are instrumental in sustaining customer engagement and loyalty over the long term. The next section will delve into practical strategies for implementing long-term nurture sequences to ensure sustained success.

The Customer Journey Framework

Awareness: The Genesis of Connection

At the very outset of the Customer Journey Framework is the **Awareness stage**. This is where potential clients first encounter your brand, perhaps through social media buzz, search engine findings, direct advertising, or word-of-mouth recommendations. It's the critical first impression, the spark that ignites interest and curiosity. Think of it as the beginning of a conversation, where your priority is to be interesting and relevant enough to invite further dialogue. Here, the content should educate and inspire, laying down the groundwork that paves the way for a deeper connection.

Consideration: Cultivating Curiosity into Interest

As curiosity evolves into serious interest, we enter the **Consideration stage**. Now your audience is weighing you against your competitors, scrutinizing your offers, and mulling over the benefits. This is your opportunity to stand out with targeted content that answers questions, provides comparisons, and addresses specific customer needs and pain points. Build this stage with content that speaks directly to your audience's considerations, like informative blogs, testimonials, and case studies that underline your unique selling proposition.

Purchase: The Moment of Commitment

The **Purchase stage** is where interest translates into action. Your prospective customers are ready to make a decision, and it is imperative that this process is as frictionless as possible. Offer clear pricing information, straightforward navigation, and reassurance such as money-back guarantees or customer support. At this junction, trust is key—it's the result of all previous nurturing efforts and is what ultimately tips the balance in favor of a conversion.

Usage: Enhancing Experience to Ensure Satisfaction

Post-purchase, the focus shifts to **Usage**. This stage is about ensuring that clients get the most out of what they've bought, which is crucial for fostering loyalty. It could involve onboarding emails, instructional videos, and responsive customer support. Above all, this stage is where value is delivered consistently; the aim is to exceed expectations, making this initial experience with your product or service memorable and satisfactory, propelling the relationship forward.

Advocacy: Empowering Customers to Be Your

Champions

Finally comes the stage of **Advocacy**. When customers not only return but also recommend you to others, they become powerful brand ambassadors. This is the pinnacle of customer engagement, achieved through exceptional service and meaningful connection. It's here that you can leverage reviews, referrals, and user-generated content to further elevate your brand. Encourage this advocacy with loyalty programs, community-focused events, or special acknowledgments for your most vocal supporters.

Connecting the Framework Dots

Understanding the individual stages is just the beginning; seeing how they intertwine is where the magic happens. Your long-term nurture sequences should aim to create a seamless journey from one stage to the next. A customer who has just discovered you on social media might need a different approach than one who's pondering a second purchase. By mapping the customer journey, you ensure that no matter where a client is, they're receiving relevant, personalized communication that guides them gently to the next stage.

Application in Real-World Scenarios

In practice, **the Customer Journey Framework** helps businesses tailor their automation efforts to each customer's phase, making marketing efforts more efficient and poignant. For instance, automated email campaigns can be segmented based on the customer's stage, delivering tailored messages that resonate and drive action. Acknowledging a customer's previous purchase in your communication can reinforce their decision and set the stage for repeat business and referral potential.

Framework in Motion

Adapting to the dynamic nature of customer relationships is key. Regularly revisit and revise your automated sequences based on feedback, analytics, and changing market conditions. Keep in mind that customers may cycle through the stages non-linearly, and your framework should be flexible enough to cater to these shifts. Stability in a nurture sequence is all about adaptability and understanding the evolving needs of your customers as they move through different stages of their journey with you.

Onward with Customer-Centric Growth

Implementing a long-term nurture sequence using the Customer Journey Framework is not a one-time task but an ongoing pursuit. It involves constantly assessing the pulse of your audience and evolving with them. The beauty of this systematic approach is that it can grow and adapt with your business, ensuring that your marketing remains synchronized with your customer's ever-changing world.

Leverage this framework to not only streamline your sales and marketing automation but to also enrich the experience at every customer touchpoint. The result? A business that doesn't just sell, but significantly impacts the lives of its customers, encouraging a loyal following. With each part of your framework in alignment, your automated empire is positioned for **sustained engagement, growth, and success**.

Long-term nurture sequences are the lifeblood of sustaining customer loyalty and engagement. By implementing these sequences, you can ensure that your customers feel valued and understood, leading to a stronger, more enduring relationship with your brand. **Remember, it's not just about the immediate sale, it's about cultivating a lasting connection.**

Focusing on building relationships and trust over time through nurture sequences is the key to long-term success in your business. When you prioritize nurturing and engaging your audience, you create a community of loyal customers who not only advocate for your brand but also become repeat buyers. **By investing in long-term nurture sequences, you're investing in the growth and sustainability of your business.**

To implement long-term nurture sequences effectively, start by **understanding your customer's journey and needs**. Tailor your content and communication to speak directly to them at every stage. Next, **leverage automation** to deliver personalized, timely messages that resonate with your audience. Lastly, **continuously monitor and**

optimize your nurture sequences to ensure they remain relevant and effective over time.

With the implementation of long-term nurture sequences, you can see a substantial increase in customer engagement, brand loyalty, and ultimately, sales. By employing these strategies, you're setting the stage for a community of supportive, engaged customers who will promote and sustain your business for years to come.

Chapter 6: Crafting Effective Upsells and Downsells

"Upselling and downselling are not merely sales tactics; they're opportunities to build stronger relationships with your customers by consistently providing them with value."

The morning mist still clung to the verdant leaves of the pepper trees that hemmed in Sam's backyard. Cradled by the aroma of earth and fresh roast, he sat, leg bouncing under the hardwood kitchen table, his laptop casting a pale light on his intent face. Sam was no less an architect of customer experiences than his grandmother was an artisan of preserves; each jar had to be as rich in flavor as the next, a testament to tradition and toil.

With a quiet click, his spreadsheet flickered into view—columns of numbers, a digital mosaic of opportunity. These were not simply figures, they were dreams unlatched, gateways to futures unknown and prosperity hoped for. A good, better, best suite of offers; automation would be the alchemy that turned these dreams to gold.

Invisible tendrils of thought threaded through past meetings, winding their way around the flutters in his chest. "Don't just sell," his mentor had pressed with a hint of lesprit de l'escalier, "enrich the customer journey, provide value at every turn." It was clear; compelling upsells and downsells could be the masterpiece upon which his reputation hinged. Sam inhaled, the rich coffee scent bolstering his resolve.

The doorbell's chime splintered his concentration. A parcel awaited, bearing the new espresso machine — a dalliance with luxury and a mirror to his current dilemma. Maximize the moment, the conundrum whispered. Each sale was this doorstep, each product a parcel, each choice a chance to impress.

By the time the sun warmed the kitchen tiles to a toasty hue, he'd crafted the blueprint of an intricate system. Upsells that whispered of need yet unheard, downsells that comforted like an old friend's consoling hand. As the evening glow settled, a lingering scent of coffee mix with the promise of unwavering determination, would Sam's carefully constructed paths lead his customers to satisfaction as potent as the taste of his home-brewed cup?

In the crucible of commerce, how does one craft an offer irresistible in its clarity, compelling in its value, ensuring that the hand that clicks 'add to cart' does so with a heart convinced and content?

Unleash the Power of Complementary Offers

In an era of high-speed digital transactions and fleeting customer interactions, mastering the nuances of upselling and downselling is tantamount to orchestrating a symphony of growth for your business. Delving into the realm of strategic offer design is not just about padding the bottom line—it's about enriching the customer journey with value-packed alternatives that resonate with their unique preferences and needs. When done with heart and savvy, you cultivate not just purchasers but passionate advocates for your brand.

The essence of heart-centered automation lies in its ability to anticipate and respond to customer behaviors with precision and empathy. Automation isn't a cold, calculating machine—it's the conduit through which a business delivers its pulse to the customer. In orchestrating your suite of offers, a "good, better, best" approach not only presents a clear value proposition but also paves a pathway for customers to organically escalate their commitment to your offerings. At its core, this is about enhancing customer choice and satisfaction while also leveraging the scalability of automation.

Understanding the symbiotic relationship between upsells and downsells and the distinct preferences of your clientele transforms the traditional sales approach into a dynamic, customer-focused dialogue. It is a dialogue that underscores your understanding of the journey each customer undergoes, allowing for serendipitous moments where your offers align perfectly with their evolving desires. It's not just the product or service that's being elevated but the customer's entire experience with your brand.

In acquiring the **key skills to design impactful upsells and downsells**, you unlock the potential of each customer interaction. By harnessing the analytical prowess of automation, you identify the most promising opportunities for offer extensions that emphasize complementary value. Every potential upsell or downsell becomes a carefully considered pitch that elevates the customer's perspective of what's possible, often before they've even realized the need for themselves.

Discovering strategies to consistently craft winning offers necessitates an intimate understanding of your customer base. This chapter is a deep dive into analyzing customer data, discerning patterns, and personalizing your strategy not just to sell more but to serve better. The strategies you'll learn here are not based on happenstance but are the result of analyzing countless interactions, running meticulously designed tests, and applying the insights gleaned from your community.

The Art of Engagement: Cultivating Your Garden of Leads

Every flourishing community has one thing in common: a nurturing environment where each member can thrive. Your automated empire is no exception. It needs a robust **lead nurturing strategy** underpinning the connections you foster. Let's embark on a step-by-step journey to transform your prospective leads into engaged, loyal customers, and in doing so, bloom a vibrant community.

Step 1: Define Your Buyer Personas

The first step involves crafting personas that are more than mere caricatures of your audience—they are the bedrock upon which personalized marketing campaigns are sculpted. Dive deep into the psyche of your customer, understand their aspirations, fears, and lifestyle. *Who are they?* More importantly, *why do they need you?*

Step 2: Map Out the Customer Journey

With personas in hand, sketch the map of their quest for solutions—your solutions. At each juncture, be the sage that provides wisdom, not the vendor pushing wares. Align your tactics with their milestones, and ensure every interaction adds a layer of trust and value to the customer narrative.

Step 3: Create Valuable Content

Content here is king, queen, and the royal court—reigning supreme over the hearts and minds of your community. Cultivate a library of content that resonates, educates, and empowers. Spin the fabric of your content calendar with care, ensuring each thread complements the next.

Step 4: Leverage Marketing Automation Tools

Automation tools are your silent sentinels, ever-watchful, ever-ready to deliver personalized experiences consistently. Deploy these digital emissaries wisely, orchestrating a symphony of timely and relevant engagements that sing to the individual tune of each lead.

Step 5: Score and Segment Your Leads

Scoring leads is akin to identifying the nutrient-rich soil in your garden of prospects. Segment these leads to tailor the growth conditions—some need the gentle touch of periodic emails; others thrive with the robust engagement of webinars and direct calls.

Step 6: Implement Multi-Channel Nurturing Campaigns

Spread the tendrils of your engagement across channels, ensuring you're present wherever your customers bloom. Synchronize your efforts to create a seamless experience that feels less like a corporate strategy and more like a companionship that walks the journey with them.

Step 7: Establish Relationship-Building Touchpoints

In nurturing, as in life, relationships are paramount. It's not just the content but the context and the connection that it fosters. Establish touchpoints that quietly whisper, "We understand and care."

Step 8: Measure and Optimize Your Lead Nurturing Campaigns

What's a garden without regular tending? Analyze, adapt, and fine-tune your nurturing strategies. Each metric is a window to better understanding—let the data illuminate the path to continuous and flourishing engagement.

Within these nurturing steps lies the power to transform interest into dedication and casual visits into enduring memberships. With heart-centered marketing at its core, the success of your automated empire is not measured in transactions but in the depth and vigor of its community.

Crafting upsells and downsells that complement each other is a crucial aspect of maximizing customer value in your sales and marketing automation system. When done effectively, these additional offers can significantly increase revenue while enhancing the overall customer experience. Understanding the importance of this strategic approach will empower you to design a seamless sequence of offers that engage and delight your customers, leading to improved loyalty and increased profitability for your business.

By carefully crafting a suite of offers that align with the needs and desires of your customers, you can create a progression of value that encourages them to invest further in your products or services. This step-wise approach not only enhances their overall experience but also presents them with opportunities to derive more value from their initial purchase. Drawing on industry insights and data-backed practices, you can design upsells and downsells that consistently deliver results, fostering a sense of fulfillment for both you and your customers.

Moreover, effective upsells and downsells can contribute to the nurturing aspect of your automation system. When these offers are strategically aligned and seamlessly integrated, they demonstrate to your customers that you understand their needs and are committed to providing tailored solutions. This fosters a sense of trust and reliability, further strengthening the relationship with your customers and setting the stage for enhanced engagement and long-term loyalty.

Combining enticing upsells and helpful downsells in a strategic manner creates a win-win situation for both you and your customers. You increase the lifetime value of each customer while providing them with options to explore and expand their engagement with your brand. This approach not only boosts your revenue but also enriches the customer journey, emphasizing the customer-centric nature of your business.

As we delve deeper into the art of crafting effective upsells and downsells, you'll discover strategies for consistently designing offers that work harmoniously to maximize customer value. By aligning these offers with the needs and preferences of your audience, you will be able to create a dynamic and lucrative suite of products and services that enhance the overall customer experience. So, let's continue our exploration and uncover the key skills in designing a good, better, best suite of offers to increase revenue through automation.

Crafting a good, better, best suite of offers is essential for increasing revenue through automation. Not only does this approach cater to various customer preferences and budgets, but it also ensures that each upsell or downsell enhances the overall customer experience. To design a suite of offers effectively, it's crucial to understand the key skills involved and how they align with the broader goal of maximizing customer value through automation.

First and foremost, **understanding customer needs and preferences** is vital. This includes conducting thorough market research, analyzing customer feedback, and keeping a close eye on industry trends. By gaining insights into what your customers truly value and desire, you can tailor your good, better, best offers to meet their exact needs.

Once you have a clear understanding of your customers' preferences, the next step is to **create a value ladder** that guides them through a natural progression of offers. The good, better, best framework allows you to offer a variety of options, ensuring that customers at different stages of their journey with your business can find a suitable and appealing offer.

Each offer within the good, better, best suite should provide **incremental value**. This means that the better and best offers should build upon the foundation of the good offer, offering additional features, benefits, or solutions to further meet the customer's needs. This progression creates a sense of growth and development in the customer's experience, enticing them to move up the ladder.

Another crucial skill in designing a good, better, best suite of offers is **aligning upsells and downsells** with the customer's journey. This ensures that each offer seamlessly fits into the overall experience, whether the customer is upgrading to a better offer or considering a downsell. These offers should complement each other, providing options that cater to diverse customer situations and needs.

Moreover, it's important to **establish clear and compelling benefits** for each offer in the suite. Customers need to see the value in each offer and understand how it aligns with their goals and challenges. Communicating the specific benefits of each offer effectively creates a strong incentive for customers to consider upsells and downsells, driving revenue while enhancing their experience.

Finally, **testing and refining** the good, better, best suite of offers is an ongoing process. By collecting and analyzing data, you can gain insights into which offers are performing well and which areas may need improvement. This iterative approach ensures that the suite of offers remains appealing and effective, continuously maximizing customer value and revenue through automation.

In summary, designing a good, better, best suite of offers involves understanding customer needs, creating a progression of value, providing incremental benefits, aligning upsells and downsells, communicating compelling benefits, and continually refining the offers. By mastering these key skills, you can create a suite of offers that not only increases revenue through automation but also enhances the overall customer experience, ultimately leading to a thriving and loyal customer community.

To maximize customer value while ensuring consistent sales growth, one effective strategy is to implement a **tiered approach** to upsells and downsells. Begin by analyzing your core offerings. Understand what makes them appealing and identify complementary products or services that enhance or augment the customer experience. For every principal product or service you offer, consider creating secondary and tertiary options that offer increasing degrees of value. **This tiered setup invites customers to elevate their experience** according to their needs and financial comfort.

Effective upselling hinges on timing and relevance. An upsell immediately following an initial purchase can tap into the customer's heightened interest. However, it's crucial that the additional offer is **highly relevant** to the original purchase. If a customer buys a set of kitchen knives, a logical upsell could be a high-quality cutting board or a knife maintenance kit. *This relevance confirms to the customer that you understand their needs and are proposing solutions that genuinely add value.*

For successful downsells, the goal is to retain the customer by providing them with options. If an upsell is rejected, offer a lower-priced alternative that still satisfies a related need or desire. Consider using a scalable feature model, where the basic version of a product can be enhanced with premium features. If a customer hesitates to purchase the premium model of a product, suggest the basic model, reassuring them that they can upgrade in the future. *The key is to maintain the opportunity for a sale*, albeit at a different price point, while nurturing the customer relationship.

Leverage data to inform your upsell and downsell strategies. Analyze purchasing patterns, customer feedback, and market trends to *understand what drives your customers' decisions*. Are they motivated by price, quality, convenience, or a combination thereof? Use this data to tailor your upselling and downselling tactics. For instance, during peak seasons or after launching a successful ad campaign, you may notice a trend in higher conversions for certain upsells. Capitalize on this by **automating targeted offers** that coincide with these peak times.

Upselling Through Education

Nurture your customers by educating them on the value of the upsells. Hold webinars, create informative content, or send out newsletters that provide deep insights into the benefits of the higher-tier products. *Use storytelling to illustrate the transformative potential of opting for the upsell.* For example, share success stories of how the premium service has dramatically improved other customers' experiences. Educational content can effectively drive upsells by helping customers visualize the superior outcomes they could achieve.

Customer service interaction is also a golden opportunity for upselling and downselling. **Train your support staff** to recognize opportunities where they can suggest additional products or downgrade options that better fit the customer's current situation. Empower them with the flexibility to offer personalized deals or one-time discounts that can seal the deal. This personalized touch can often tip the balance, converting a customer teetering on the edge of decision-making.

A/B testing is another vital strategy. Regularly test different upsell and downsell offers to various segments of your audience to see what resonates best. Keep a close eye on conversion rates and customer feedback - this will tell you what's working and what's not. Adjust your offers accordingly, always striving to **deliver maximum value**. Remember, the goal of your upsell and downsell strategy is to enhance customer satisfaction while also increasing the average order value.

In summary, upselling and downselling are not merely sales tactics; they're opportunities to **build stronger relationships** with your customers by consistently providing them with value. With each interaction, aim to understand and fulfill your customers' needs, and don't be afraid to innovate and evolve your approaches based on the insights you gather. By doing so, you'll create a loyal customer base that is responsive to both upsells and downsells, fuelling a steady increase in revenue over time.

Crafting effective upsells and downsells is a crucial aspect of building a successful and sustainable business. In this chapter, we have explored the significance of **crafting offers** that complement each other, the key skills in designing a **good, better, best suite** of offers, and strategies for consistently designing upsells and downsells that work to maximize **customer value**.

When it comes to offering upsells and downsells, the goal is to **maximize the value** provided to the customers while also increasing revenue through automation. By ensuring that your offers complement each other and provide real value, you are not only serving your customers better, but you are also positioning your business for growth.

Remember, the process of crafting effective upsells and downsells is **an ongoing evolution**. Pay attention to customer feedback, analyze purchasing patterns, and don't be afraid to test new ideas. The more you prioritize the needs and desires of your customers, the more successful your upsells and downsells will be.

As you move forward, keep in mind that successful automation is built on a foundation of **customer-centricity**. Always seek to provide genuine value to your customers through your upsells and downsells, and your efforts will be rewarded with **loyal, engaged customers** who continue to support your business.

In the next chapter, We will delve into the importance of **nurturing automation** and how it can help you build and maintain a loyal community of engaged customers. This is a crucial aspect of scaling your business while preserving that personal touch that sets your brand apart.

Chapter 7: Measuring Audience Behaviors for Informed Automation Strategies

" It's like having an army of digital marketers at your disposal, each one perfectly in sync with the needs and interests of a segment of your audience."

It was late afternoon when Spencer stepped into the serene quiet of his home office, the golden hue of the setting sun casting a gentle warmth over the oak desk clustered with notes and charts. The data sprawled before him spoke of behaviors and patterns, each number a voice in a choir of market trends, customer journeys, and digital footprints.

He sank into his chair, fingers drumming a slow rhythm on the polished wood. Today's meeting with the marketing team had centered on a challenge both familiar and daunting: how to harness the raw data of audience interactions, refine it into insights, and use it to bolster the company's growth. Their automation strategy was solid, yet the implementation hinged on an intricate understanding of their audience - a puzzle piece just beyond their grasp.

The quiet hum of the computer seemed to mock his uncertainty. Spencer had read countless case studies and witnessed businesses rise and fall on the strength of their data-driven decisions. The weight of potential success pressed against his ribs, a constant reminder of what could be achieved with the right analysis tools in place. He envisioned a future where every campaign was a symphony of precision, each note played to perfection by the grand orchestra of automation.

As twilight merged into evening, he paced the room, a silent ballet between fleeting shadows and whispers of thought. He recalled a conversation with an old mentor, the words now resonating with renewed urgency: "To scale a business, you must first scale your understanding of those you serve."

Tomorrow, he would begin crafting the systems to measure every click, every opened email, every paused video. With every data point, he would draw closer to the heartbeats of his audience, each one unique yet part of a larger rhythm that dictated the flow of the marketplace.

But tonight, there was solace in the simple act of contemplation, in the knowing that the path to success was paved with the very challenges that now occupied his thoughts. Spencer lingered by the window, the last light of day whispering promises of clarity and achievement.

Could the very numbers that seemed so cold and indifferent hold the secret to creating connections that were anything but?

Unlocking the Metrics of Engagement

Data is a beacon in the vast ocean of digital interaction; it navigates the trajectory of every successful business venture. Within this treasure trove, one gem shines brightest: understanding your audience's behavior. This insight is not just a tool; it is the cornerstone of creating a thriving automated empire. Yet, to truly harness this power, we must first construct the right systems to capture and interpret the vast array of data points. In this era of heart-centered marketing, fostering a massive community and scaling your business does not require sacrificing personal touch for efficiency. It calls for a delicate balance, a synergy between automation and empathy, driven by informed strategies sculpted from audience behavior analytics.

Strategic systems are vital to decipher the elusive story behind

clicks, views, and engagement metrics that form the backbone of audience data. These narratives illuminate the pathways where your marketing's heart beats in unison with your customers' needs. As we navigate this **journey of exploration**, it becomes clear that data is not just numbers on a screen but a reflection of desires waiting to be met with meaningful interactions. When these patterns are translated into actionable intelligence, you leverage automation not as a blunt instrument, but as a sculptor's chisel, carefully crafting experiences that resonate on a personal level.

Discovering the *significance of measuring audience behaviors* unfolds in layers, like unraveling the DNA of digital footprints to reveal the core of human interaction. This chapter goes beyond explaining 'what' metrics to measure, diving deep into 'how' these metrics inform every facet of your sales and marketing automation. Audience behavior data does more than shape campaigns; it's a dynamic dialogue, a feedback loop that guides nurturing efforts with precision and care.

Learning from audience data transcends mere observation. It's an active engagement where each click tells a story, and every conversion signals a deeper relationship. As the chapter unfurls, the importance of leveraging these insights becomes unmistakable. It demonstrates *how data serves as a springboard for scaling your business*, allowing you to **tailor marketing efforts** that retain human warmth despite the expansive reach of automation.

Incorporating data into strategic decisions imbues your marketing automation with relevance and empathy, underpinned by an understanding that behind every data point is a human heart. As you acquire skills to sift through the digital echoes, you glean insights that enable a connection, striking that delicate balance of efficiency within *personability* in the automated sphere.

As we conclude the introduction and segue into a more tangible application of these principles, consider the concrete steps to not only gather this vital data but to utilize it effectively in *social media advertising*, an arena that beautifully illustrates the intersection of behavior metrics and automated systems.

The Social Architect's Blueprint for Social Media Mastery

Step 1: Define Your Advertising Goals

Begin with clarity—the skeleton of any successful venture. Establish concrete goals to ensure every piece of content, every ad, is purposed with intent.

Step 2: Identify Your Target Audience

Like an archaeologist sifting for relics, comb through analytics tools to unearth the demographics and behaviors of your intended audience. Construct solid buyer personas that will stand as the foundation for targeted campaigns.

Step 3: Choose the Right Social Media Platforms

Not all terrains are equal for construction. Evaluate platform demographics and engagement patterns to position your marketing edifice on fertile ground where your audience flourishes.

Step 4: Create Compelling Ad Copy and Visuals

Your ad copy and visuals are the bricks and mortar of your advertisement building. Craft them with care to captivate and motivate, compelling viewers towards your desired action.

Step 5: Set Up Targeting and Budget Settings

Precision is key—like setting the gears of a clock. Utilize platform targeting options and define your budget with the precision of an architect ensuring the longevity of their creation.

Step 6: Monitor and Optimize Your Campaigns

With your ads live, your role shifts to that of a vigilant overseer. Monitor performance metrics and optimize, adapting as one does to the ever-shifting winds of market preference.

Step 7: Retarget Your Audience

Even the most splendid structures need reinforcement. Retarget individuals who showed initial interest to reinforce connections and solidify conversions.

Step 8: Analyze, Learn, and Iterate

Analyzing campaign data provides the blueprints for future constructions. Learn from the insights gathered to refine and evolve your strategies through continuous iteration.

The art of digital audience measurement married to the science of marketing automation is not just about crafting a towering empire; it's about constructing a home for a community that gathers around shared values and mutual respect. Through meticulously measuring audience behaviors, leveraging this bounty of insight, and blending it with the human-centric approach of heart-centered marketing, you sketch the future of a business that thrives on both scales and soul.

Have you ever wondered how successful businesses seem to anticipate their audience's needs and preferences almost effortlessly? One crucial secret lies in creating systems to measure audience behaviors for informed decision-making in automation. As a business owner, understanding your audience's behaviors can be a game-changer, allowing you to tailor your marketing and nurturing efforts while leveraging automation to scale your business. Each behavior, click, and engagement is like a breadcrumb leading you to a deeper understanding of your audience, which is essential for building a thriving community of engaged customers.

Understanding the significance of measuring audience behaviors empowers you to design smart automation strategies that are not only efficient but also deeply personalized. When you know exactly what your audience responds to, you're better equipped to deliver relevant and valuable content that resonates with them. The data you collect from audience behaviors serves as a goldmine for scaling a business, allowing you to make informed decisions, craft tailored marketing strategies, and nurture leads effectively. By implementing systems to measure audience behaviors, you're positioning your business for consistent growth and long-term success.

Data on audience behaviors isn't just about numbers and graphs; it's about understanding the people behind the data. Each click, open rate, or social media interaction represents a real person showing interest in your brand. When you analyze these behaviors, you gain valuable insights into what makes your audience tick. Armed with this knowledge, you can create personalized experiences and tailor your automation strategies to meet the unique needs of your audience. This level of personalization builds trust and strengthens the bond between your brand and your customers.

Informed decision-making in automation strategies begins with a deep understanding of your audience's behaviors. By identifying patterns in their interactions with your brand, you can predict their preferences and anticipate their needs. This level of insight allows you to automate your marketing and sales processes in a way that feels personalized and authentic. As a result, your audience feels understood and valued, leading to increased engagement, loyalty, and ultimately, a thriving community of customers who are genuinely invested in your brand.

Measuring audience behaviors is not just about collecting data; it's about using that data to inform your strategy and drive results. With the right systems in place, you'll be able to measure the effectiveness of your automation efforts, identify areas for improvement, and optimize your processes for even greater success. This data-driven approach to automation isn't just about efficiency; it's about creating meaningful connections with your audience and nurturing those connections to build a loyal and engaged community.

Understanding the significance of measuring

audience behaviors will transform your approach to automation strategies. Let's explore how data on audience behaviors serves as a valuable resource for informed decision-making in nurturing efforts.

Data on audience behaviors is a goldmine for informed decision-making in nurturing efforts. By understanding how your audience engages with your content, you can tailor your marketing and nurturing strategies to better meet their needs. What's more, this valuable data allows you to create more targeted and personalized interactions, ultimately leading to stronger connections with your audience.

Measuring Audience Behaviors

Gathering data on audience behaviors involves tracking metrics such as website visits, clicks, social media interactions, and email open rates. Understanding these behaviors can provide deep insights into what resonates with your audience, allowing you to focus on the most meaningful and impactful actions.

Leveraging Data for Informed Nurturing Strategies

When armed with data on audience behaviors, you can segment your audience based on their interactions. This segmentation allows for tailored and targeted nurturing efforts. For instance, you can design specific email campaigns for different segments based on their engagement levels, ensuring that your messages are relevant and compelling to each group.

Personalizing the Customer Experience

Data on audience behaviors also empowers you to create a more personalized customer experience. By knowing the content that resonates with different segments of your audience, you can deliver highly relevant and personalized interactions. For example, you can recommend specific products based on their previous interactions or personalize the content they see on your website.

Fueling Informed Content Creation

By analyzing audience behaviors, you can gain valuable insights into the type of content that best resonates with your audience. This data can guide your content creation strategy, helping you produce more of the content that your audience finds engaging. It ensures that your content is always relevant and valuable to your audience.

Building Stronger Relationships

The ability to understand your audience's behaviors allows you to build stronger relationships with them. By delivering personalized and relevant content, you demonstrate that you understand and care about their needs. This creates a sense of trust and loyalty, leading to long-term, meaningful relationships with your audience.

Enhancing Marketing Efficiency

When nurturing efforts are informed by data on audience behaviors, your marketing efforts become more efficient. Instead of taking a one-size-fits-all approach, you can direct your resources toward the strategies and tactics that are most effective in engaging your audience. This results in better returns on your marketing investments.

Driving Conversion and Sales

Ultimately, data on audience behaviors plays a pivotal role in driving conversions and sales. By nurturing your audience based on their behaviors, you can guide them through the buyer's journey more effectively, increasing the likelihood of conversion. This targeted approach to nurturing ultimately leads to higher sales and increased customer satisfaction.

Informed decision-making in nurturing efforts relies heavily on data on audience behaviors. By leveraging this data to create targeted, personalized interactions, businesses can build stronger relationships, enhance marketing efficiency, and ultimately drive conversions and sales.

Harnessing the Power of Data to Scale Your Business

The lifeblood of scaling your business lies in **data-driven insights**. When you meticulously track and assess audience behaviors, you not only gain clarity on what drives engagement and conversion but also the knowledge to implement intelligent automation that feels personal and effective. Consider every click, view, and interaction as a treasure trove of information, preparing you to sharpen your marketing strategies and streamline your automation processes. This data allows you to anticipate needs and build systems that deliver value at scale, ensuring no lead is left unattended and each customer feels seen and understood.

Making Marketing Personal with Automation

Imagine a marketing campaign that adapts to each potential customer's actions and preferences. Leveraging detailed data on audience behaviors, you can craft automation sequences that respond dynamically to each individual's journey with your brand. It's like having an army of digital marketers at your disposal, each one perfectly in sync with the needs and interests of a segment of your audience. This capability doesn't just elevate the efficacy of your marketing; it revolutionizes the very fabric of customer engagement. The intelligent use of automation, fueled by meticulous data analysis, enables you to serve your audience the content they crave at the optimal moment, dramatically boosting conversion rates.

Building Intuitive Nurturing Systems

As your understanding of audience data deepens, you can deploy nurturing systems that foster relationships and build trust on autopilot. From the welcoming email that hits a new subscriber's inbox to the timely follow-up with a hesitant shopper, every automated touchpoint is crafted with precision based on real behavior trends. This strategic nurturing not only elevates the customer experience but also streamlines operations, freeing up your time to focus on innovation and growth. By integrating audience behavior data into your nurturing systems, you make every marketing dollar work harder, turning insights into outcomes that reflect on your bottom line.

The Synergy of Scalability and Customization

Scaling a business doesn't mean losing the human touch; on the contrary, it offers an opportunity to personalize interactions at a level one-to-one efforts can't match. The right data sets the stage for automation tools to create a symphony of personalized experiences for masses of individuals simultaneously. The key lies in segmenting your audience based on their behaviors and curating content that speaks directly to each segment. This strategy not only enhances the customer journey but also gives you the leverage to scale with a personal touch that fosters loyalty and advocacy.

Realizing Growth Through Measurable Results

In the digital age, success is quantifiable. Through detailed audience metrics, **your business's growth trajectory becomes crystal clear**. Such insights empower you to invest in the most impactful marketing channels and refine strategies real-time. As you fine-tune your automation systems, you'll see customer acquisition costs decrease and lifetime value soar. This is not just a matter of financial prudence but a strategic imperative for sustainable growth in an increasingly competitive marketplace.

Anticipating Market Changes with Predictive Analytics

Implementing advanced analytics into your strategy translates to forecasting the future needs of your market and preparing to meet them head-on. Audience behavior data can predict trends and identify patterns that would otherwise go unnoticed. Tools that analyze and learn from your audience enable you to *stay ahead of the curve*, adapt your marketing, and optimize automations for peak performance. Such foresight is your defense against market volatility, keeping your business agile and proactive rather than reactive.

Customer Lifetime Value and Retention Focus

Focusing on customer retention is as critical as acquisition, if not more so. Tracking how customers interact with your brand over time illuminates pathways to increase their lifetime value. Implementing automation that recognizes customer milestones, rewards loyalty, and provides value with each interaction ensures customers not only stay but become enthusiastic supporters of your brand. These customers are your greatest asset, and the data-driven nurturing strategies you develop through automation can turn satisfactory service into remarkable experiences that keep them coming back for more.

Leveraging Feedback Loops for Continuous Improvement

The journey of a customer within your business ecosystem is a source of continuous learning. By establishing feedback loops that capture and analyze customer interactions, you position your business to evolve continuously. This cycle of measuring, analyzing, and adjusting your automation strategies creates a self-improving system that enhances customer satisfaction while driving efficiency and growth. It's a proactive approach that ensures every aspect of your marketing and sales automation is a robust, living process that matures with your business and market needs.

Each data point collected from your audience provides vital insights for informed decision-making. By understanding and implementing *tailored marketing efforts* through informed automation, businesses can offer compelling, personalized experiences that resonate with their audience and drive loyalty. As you continue to refine your approach and embrace the potential of data, remember this endeavor is not about replacing the human element—it's about amplifying it with the precision and scale that today's technological tools afford.

Scaling your business empire demands vigilance, agility, and the willingness to continually adapt. Smart automation driven by audience data is the compass that guides you through the complex terrain of market dynamics. As you chart your course with this compass in hand, the path to a thriving business—one that grows not just in size but in depth of customer relationships—becomes ever clearer.

As we wrap up this chapter, it's clear that **measuring audience behaviors is the cornerstone of an effective automation strategy**. Data on audience behaviors allows for informed decision-making in nurturing efforts and tailoring marketing strategies, ultimately leading to business growth and scalability.

By implementing systems to measure audience behaviors, businesses can gain valuable insights that inform their automation strategies. This data empowers businesses to make informed decisions in their nurturing efforts, ensuring that they are providing personalized and relevant content to their audience. Moreover, by leveraging this data, businesses can tailor their marketing efforts to suit the specific needs and preferences of their audience, ultimately creating a more engaging and effective marketing strategy.

It's crucial for businesses to recognize the significance of data in scaling their operations and leveraging automation for tailored marketing efforts. With the right data at their fingertips, businesses can implement automation strategies that not only save time and resources but also build stronger relationships with their audience. This leads to not just increased efficiency, but also a more personalized and nurturing customer experience.

In the next chapter, we will delve into the practical steps of leveraging this data to design and implement automation strategies that are both efficient and nurturing. We'll explore how to put this valuable audience behavior data to use in automating marketing and sales processes, so stay tuned for actionable insights and step-by-step guidance.

Chapter 8: Amplifying Personality in Marketing for Attraction and Repulsion

"This isn't about being liked by everyone; it's about being loved by the right ones."

The small-town cafe buzzed with the soothing hum of idle conversation and the clinking of porcelain. Among the patrons, James, a local entrepreneur with a small but passionate following, sat pondering over a steaming cup of coffee. His eyes, reflecting a deep-seated determination, were fixed on his laptop screen, though his mind wandered far beyond.

Today's task was daunting, yet full of potential: to infuse his marketing with an authenticity and personality that would resonate with the right customers. He remembered an article he'd read, echoing in his mind—that the essence of a brand lay in its authenticity and unique character. A brand that's too generic or impersonal, it argued, lacks the charm to create lasting bonds with customers.

James's gaze drifted to the world outside the window, where people strode by, each their own protagonist in a myriad of unfolding stories. It struck him then, an epiphany wrapped in the mundane—a sense of identity could attract or repel, much like the resonant frequency of glass. The idea was to amplify his own frequency, his brand's true voice, to shatter the barriers between his products and his true audience.

Returning to his laptop, James's fingers danced across the keys, crafting messages that bore his ideals, personal tales that embodied his values. He penned an anecdote about the origins of his passion project, felt the warm glow of nostalgia, and the twinge of fear at sharing such intimate details with the world.

The aroma of freshly ground coffee mingled with the scent of rain that had started to pat against the windows, grounding him. He gleaned strategies from somewhere deep within, some gathered from experts, others from his triumphs and failures. From customer testimonials to sincere stories of struggle, each piece was a crafted testament to the journey of his brand.

His heart thrummed in anticipation. By revealing the heart of his business, by being vulnerable and true, would he invite kindred spirits into his fold? Or would he inadvertently push away the onlookers not meant for this narrative?

It was a delicate balance, shaping a conversation that could either whittle down his audience to its core or expand its horizons to unforeseen breadths. There was no certainty, only the promise of authenticity as a compass, guiding his choices.

As the day waned and the cafe emptied, the question hung in the air, pregnant with potential: How might others discover their authentic voice within the market's clamor, and what marvels could that voice unveil for their brands and their lives?

Magnetize Your Tribe: The Personality Principle

Marketing is not just about showcasing your product; it's about illuminating your brand's soul. Every tweet, every email, every tagline is a reflection of who you are and what you stand for. In the realm of **heart-centered marketing**, injecting your unique personality into your brand isn't just a creative exercise—it's a strategic necessity. We're entering an age where **authenticity reigns supreme** and where the best filter for an ideal audience is a bold statement of identity.

Your brand's personality is the beacon that attracts those who resonate with your **core values** and the shield that repels those who do not. As we explore this chapter, you'll understand why **authenticity** is not just the latest buzzword—it's the cornerstone of a magnetic marketing strategy. Remember, attracting the right crowd is as valuable as dissuading the not-so-right, ensuring that your community comprises individuals truly aligned with your mission.

Let's dissect the three dimensions of personality in marketing—attraction, repulsion, and engagement. By understanding these elements, you'll gain insights into crafting a persona that doesn't just echo trends but speaks directly to the hearts of your prospective community. This isn't about being liked by everyone; it's about being loved by the right ones.

Strategy Over Serendipity: Crafting Your Personality Blueprint

Laying the groundwork for a **personality-infused brand** requires deliberate action. It's not about leaving impressions to chance; it's about architecting experiences that resonate. Learn techniques to integrate your brand's authentic voice consistently across all platforms. These actionable steps ensure that your audience not only hears but feels the essence of your brand, fostering a deeper connection.

Moving beyond theory, we dive into the practical application of **repelling the misaligned**. This might seem counterintuitive in a world that obsesses over numbers, but repulsion is a secret weapon. It conserves your energy and resources for those who truly matter—your advocates, your loyal customers, your tribe. By honing your message, you filter out noise and make way for a **harmonious symphony** of client relationships.

The Engagement Equation: Interactive Authenticity

Authentic engagement is the lifeblood of a thriving online community. Discover strategies that transform passive observers into active participants, creating a dynamic interchange between you and your audience. Engagement is a two-way street—a dialogue that enriches both the giver and the receiver. Implement these tactics, and watch as your community evolves from a crowd of onlookers to a chorus of brand champions.

Stepping into the arena with a bold, authentic brand personality is both an art and science. It's about understanding your identity, communicating it effectively, and then refining it through connection with your audience. Each tweet, every product launch, each customer interaction is an opportunity to reinforce who you are.

By the end of this chapter, you'll have crafted a brand so **vibrant and true** to itself that the right people can't help but be drawn in. And when those who don't fit find their way to other tribes, you'll acknowledge it as part of the process. With these insights and tools, prepare to build a community that's not just big—but bound together by the indelible bonds of shared values and vision.

In the world of marketing, authenticity and personality are like magnets that attract the right audience while repelling the wrong ones. When a brand infuses its marketing efforts with genuine authenticity and a distinctive personality, it creates a powerful pull for its ideal customers, drawing them in with a message and a vibe that resonates. This not only fosters more meaningful and engaged relationships but also serves another purpose: it filters out customers who may not align with the brand's values and offerings.

By infusing authenticity and personality into marketing, a brand speaks directly to the hearts of its ideal audience. It's like having a conversation with a friend who understands and shares the same values and beliefs. This authenticity appeals to the emotions, building trust and forming a deeper connection. The result? A loyal following that becomes an advocate for the brand, promoting it to others and creating a community built on shared values and experiences.

But in addition to drawing in the right audience, infusing authenticity and personality into marketing also serves as a filtering mechanism. It creates a clear signal to those who may not resonate with the brand's personality or message, naturally repelling them. This is a strategic move to ensure that the brand attracts not just any customers, but the right ones—those who will actively engage, remain loyal, and become brand ambassadors. In essence, by being true to itself, a brand not only attracts but also repels, ensuring that its community is aligned in values and spirit.

Achieving this balance of attraction and repulsion through authenticity and personality isn't just a marketing tactic; it's a strategic decision that shapes the foundation of the brand's community. It means the difference between attracting a large, yet disengaged, transient audience and cultivating a small, devoted, and enthusiastic community that sustains growth and success over the long term.

To truly understand the impact of infusing authenticity and personality into marketing for attracting the right audience, we must delve deeper into the practical strategies behind this approach. In the following section, we'll explore how these strategies can be implemented to communicate the brand's values and personality effectively, fostering genuine connections with the ideal audience. Keep reading to discover how to amplify the unique elements of your brand and build a community of engaged customers who share your vision.

In marketing, personality serves as a powerful filter, repelling customers who may not align with the brand's values and offerings. By amplifying the brand's personality, businesses can actively repel the wrong customers, creating a more focused and engaged audience. This deliberate repulsion is not about driving potential customers away; rather, it is about establishing a clear identity and value system to attract the right individuals. **When your marketing efforts are infused with authenticity and personality, they naturally attract like-minded customers while simultaneously turning away those who may not resonate with your brand.**

Understanding Your Ideal Customer

Before delving into how to repel customers who may not align with your brand, it's crucial to have a clear understanding of your ideal customer.

Who are the individuals that resonate with your brand's personality, values, and offerings? What are their interests, pain points, and aspirations? By defining your ideal customer persona with precision, you can better tailor your marketing efforts to attract and engage the right audience. **This targeted approach ensures that your brand's personality appeals to those who are most likely to become loyal and engaged customers.**

Repelling Misaligned Customers

While many businesses focus on attracting customers, repelling those who don't align with the brand is equally important. The amplification of personality in marketing allows businesses to communicate their values, beliefs, and unique characteristics clearly. **By doing so, they naturally repel customers who do not resonate with their brand's identity.** Whether it's through bold statements, authentic storytelling, or distinct visual elements, the amplified personality serves as a beacon, attracting the right customers while repelling those who may not be a good fit.

Why Repulsion Is Essential

Repelling customers who don't align with the brand may seem counterintuitive at first glance. However, it is an essential step in building a loyal and engaged audience. When your marketing efforts are designed to attract a broad, undefined audience, you may end up with customers who don't truly connect with your brand's values and offerings. **This can lead to a disengaged customer base and a diluted brand identity. By actively repelling misaligned customers, you ensure that your audience is genuinely enthusiastic about what your brand stands for.**

Amplifying Personality Through Authenticity

To effectively repel misaligned customers, the amplification of personality must be rooted in authenticity. When your marketing is genuine and true to your brand's essence, it naturally communicates your identity, values, and offerings to the right audience. **By staying true to your brand, you naturally draw in those who resonate with your authenticity and drive away those who don't.** This ensures that your customer base is not only engaged but also committed to your brand's vision and mission.

Consistency in Personality Amplification

Consistency is key when amplifying your brand's personality for repulsion. It's not a one-time effort but an ongoing process that permeates your marketing strategies, communications, and customer interactions. From the tone of your content to the design of your brand materials, every touchpoint should echo your brand's unique personality. **By consistently amplifying your brand's personality, you reinforce its identity, attracting the right customers, and repelling those who don't align with your values and offerings.**

Creating Meaningful Relationships

By repelling misaligned customers, businesses are able to focus their efforts on cultivating meaningful relationships with the right audience. This targeted approach allows for deeper connections, more impactful engagements, and a community of loyal customers. **When your brand's personality repels those who don't align with its values, you create space for genuine, meaningful relationships with those who do.**

By understanding the impact of infusing authenticity and personality into marketing for both attraction and repulsion, businesses can forge a more meaningful connection with their ideal audience while filtering out customers who may not align with their brand's values and offerings. The amplification of personality serves as a powerful tool for attracting the right customers and repelling the wrong ones, ultimately leading to more engaged relationships and a more focused customer base.

The Power of Lead Scoring

Within the bustling digital marketplace, the ability to discern not just who your leads are, but how likely they are to blossom into paying customers, is the cornerstone of an efficient marketing strategy. Enter the "Lead Scoring Model," an analytical framework designed for the modern marketer to optimize lead prioritization and nurturing efforts. Below, we unfold the layers of this model and impart strategies for integrating authenticity and personality into your marketing, nurturing meaningful customer relationships.

Lead Engagement Criteria: The Beacon of Interest

At its core, the Lead Scoring Model starts with understanding the depth of a potential customer's interactions with your brand. Engagement criteria serve as metrics that signal a lead's interest level. These might include how often a lead opens marketing emails, the frequency of clicks on links within these emails, duration and recency of website visits, participation in webinars, and responses to calls-to-action such as filling out forms or downloading resources.

Assigning point values to each criterion is a craft—choosing numbers that reflect the engagement's significance. For example, attending a live webinar might score higher than opening an email, as it indicates a higher investment of a lead's time and interest. As you infuse personality into your marketing content and platforms, watch how engagement criteria shift. Authenticity can often surge engagement scores, illustrating the magnetic pull of a brand that resonates on a human level.

Lead Scoring Formula: Calculating Potential

With the engagement criteria set, each interaction a lead has with your brand fills their scorecard. The lead scoring formula is the alchemist's equation that transmutes these points into a golden insight—the lead's overall score. This formula must consider the weighted values of each type of engagement to derive a score that not only signifies a lead's current engagement level but also predicts their likelihood of conversion.

As you incorporate your unique brand personality into marketing tactics, the lead scoring formula adapts, becoming more refined and tailored to the types of customers you aim to attract. Higher scores earmark leads that are not just interacting but doing so in ways that suggest they align with your brand's voice and values. Here is where your personable content proves its mettle, moving from mere touchpoints to potential conversions.

The Interplay of Criteria and Scoring

Each component of the Lead Scoring Model is interdependent. Without robust engagement criteria, the scoring formula would lack the nuance required to segment leads effectively. Similarly, without an articulate formula, the rich data from engagement criteria would not translate into actionable intelligence.

This synergy between criteria and formula is dynamic—constantly evolving with every campaign, each piece of content, and the ongoing dialog with your audience. When your marketing pulse beats with authenticity, this interplay harmonizes, fine-tuning who to focus your attention on for the greatest mutual benefit.

Practical Implications

The practicality of the Lead Scoring Model is its beacon. By integrating this framework into your marketing automation, you ensure that resources are invested in leads who are genuinely captivated by your brand's personality. This model functions as a bridge between data-driven strategies and the human touch that defines heart-centered marketing.

As you bring your brand's personality to the fore, you may find that lead behaviors—and thus, scores—begin to lean heavily towards those who share your brand ethos. This alignment is no coincidence; it's the manifestation of a successfully amplified personality resonating with its intended audience.

The Lead Scoring Model in Motion

Over time, the Lead Scoring Model not only illuminates which leads are becoming more engaged but also how changes in your marketing strategy impact lead behavior. For instance, a campaign that deeply embodies your brand's values might create ripples through your scoring, with a noticeable uptick in high-value leads. This feedback loop becomes essential for understanding the true impact of marketing with authenticity and honing in on strategies that yield the most fertile engagements.

Examining these shifts over time paints a picture of how well your brand's personality is being received and where there's room for enhancement. It's not just about the initial attraction; it's about fostering on-going conversations and deepening relationships with a community aligned with your vision.

Toward Meaningful Engagements

By meticulously scoring leads based on the criteria that reflect genuine engagement and potential alignment with your brand, you can focus on nurturing the relationships that matter most. Articulating your brand's character through each marketing channel becomes a harmonious effort that naturally attracts like-minded individuals.

This framework isn't just about efficiency; it's about cultivating a space where your brand's unique personality thrives and resonates. With the Lead Scoring Model as your guide, you streamline your focus towards fostering connections that have the potential to grow into a loyal and engaged community.

Through this process, not only do your sales and marketing efforts become more targeted and fruitful, but the entire ethos of your Automated Empire is defined by relationships that are both meaningful and genuine. Each lead becomes not just a number but a narrative—a journey of engagement with your brand's authentic voice at its heart.

In amplifying personality in your marketing efforts, the goal is not just to attract customers, but to attract the right customers. By infusing your brand with authenticity and personality, you create a magnetic pull for the ideal audience, leading to more meaningful and engaged relationships. This process is not just about drawing people in, but also about repelling those who may not align with your brand's values and offerings. **This strategic approach to marketing helps in filtering out customers who are not the right fit, saving time and resources while focusing on nurturing the relationships that truly matter.**

When you're authentic and upfront about your brand's personality, you establish a clear identity that resonates with those who share similar values and interests. This leads to a deeper connection with your audience, as they see themselves reflected in your brand. **This bond can become the cornerstone of a loyal community of engaged customers who are not just buying a product or service, but buying into a meaningful relationship with your brand.**

We've learned that infusing authenticity and personality into marketing involves a strategic blend of storytelling, genuine interaction, and consistent messaging. **By sharing your brand story in an engaging way, you provide your audience with a deeper understanding of who you are and what you stand for. By consistently exhibiting your brand's personality through all communication touchpoints, you reinforce your identity and attract like-minded individuals. And by genuinely interacting with your audience, you cultivate trust and authenticity, laying the foundation for long-lasting relationships.**

As you move forward, keep in mind that this process is not about appealing to everyone. It's about appealing to the right people. **Embrace the fact that not everyone will resonate with your brand, and understand that it's okay to repel those who don't align with your values and offerings. In doing so, you'll free up your resources to focus on nurturing the relationships that truly matter, creating a community of loyal customers who champion your brand and contribute to its growth.**

In the next chapter, we'll delve into actionable strategies for nurturing these meaningful relationships and building a loyal community of engaged customers.

Now, let's take the next step towards fostering an authentic and resonant brand.

Chapter 9: Creating a Highly Efficient Nurturing Automation System

"Nurturing automation and heart-centered marketing act as twin engines propelling your business forward on autopilot, without compromising on the integrity of customer relationships."

A gentle breeze rustled through the leaves, infusing the air with the promise of rain as Emma stood amidst the rows of lavender in her family's herb farm. It was here, in this late afternoon with the sun painting the horizon in hues of amber and rose, where she pondered upon nurturing automation and heart-centered marketing, the twin beacons that could steer her small business to embrace the horizon.

Her family's business, once thriving on the palpable human touch, now needed to scale, to reach hearts afar without losing the soul woven into their craft. Emma recalled the fondness in her customers' voices, the look of tranquility dawning upon faces as they'd breathe in the balmy scents of her products. She needed that essence captured, replicated across digital waves, yet the fear of diluting her brand's sincerity with automation gnawed at her.

As her hands softly brushed against the fragrant petals, her thoughts spiraled. How could she maintain the warmth of personal connection when her voice had to travel through the calculated clicks of an automated system? It was a strategy she mused could very well decode her desire to scale without becoming just another faceless entity. A system built on the foundations of nurturance and heart.

She envisioned emails that didn't merely 'ping' with offers, but whispered stories into the inboxes, stories of her grandmother planting the first seeds, her father nurturing the blooms. And each tale, while part of an automated sequence, would carry a piece of her family's legacy, an invitation to be part of a story that grew and thrived, much like the herbs under the tender watch of the sun and rain.

The day faded, the dusk encroaching with a subtle chill. But her heart was ablaze, ideas fusing like constellations in a clear night sky. She imagined a marketing system not as a cold mechanical entity, but as an extension of their farm's handshake, a digital smile gracing someone's day. The trick, she knew, lay in the alchemy of infusing technology with the heartbeat of her brand.

Emma watched the light retreat, the moon casting long shadows over the earth. The challenge before her seemed less daunting now, as crickets began their nightly serenade. Was it possible, she wondered, to chart a course that married efficiency with empathy? Could her hands sow seeds not just in the soil, but in the algorithms and automations that would nurture relationships across continents?

And as the stars blinked above, a thought rippled through her, gentle yet resonant—isn't the true art of business nurturing growth while holding hands with the very soul that sparked its beginnings?

Embrace Nurturing Automation: The Heartbeat of Growth

Embarking on the journey to scale your business is thrilling, yet dotted with unseen challenges. It necessitates a paradigm shift in customer relations—a fusion of high-touch with high-tech. **Nurturing automation harbors the power to streamline repetitive tasks while bringing a personalized approach to each customer interaction.** Above all, tapping into nurturing automation spearheads efficiency and primes your enterprise for exponential growth.

To cultivate a thriving community around your brand—built on the foundations of connection and empathy—you need more than sophisticated tools; you need a nurtured heart. This is where heart-centered marketing comes in, ensuring that your automated systems don't forgo the human touch your audience craves. **Efficiency in automation, combined with the warmth of human-centric communication, creates a potent vehicle for fostering loyalty and trust among your customer base.**

Understanding the significant role nurturing automation and heart-centered marketing play in business scalability is critical. They act as twin engines propelling your business forward on autopilot, without compromising on the integrity of customer relationships. This chapter is steeped in the wisdom of streamlining your operations while simultaneously kindling the kind of connections that convert customers into brand evangelists.

Learning how to seamlessly integrate automation with genuine customer engagement can be transformative. It's about striking a delicate balance that respects the individuality of each lead while serving them en masse. It isn't a zero-sum game; rather, **it's the art of personalization at scale.** Achieving this balance isn't merely a luxury—it's a competitive necessity in today's market, dominated by discerning consumers who demand relevance and care in every interaction.

Discovering strategic methods to create and implement a nurturing automation system is pivotal. This ensures your marketing is not only heard but felt—resonating deeply with the needs and aspirations of your audience. It involves crafting messages that speak directly to the individual, using data to inform and empathy to connect, weaving a narrative that aligns with their journey and amplifies their experience with your brand.

Practical, actionable advice is the cornerstone of our exploration. You'll glean strategies that can be put into practice immediately, transforming abstract concepts into actionable steps. These insights are culled from evidence-based practices and real-world successes, providing you with a blueprint to craft an automated system that resonates authenticity.

Nothing about nurturing automation and heart-centered marketing has to be esoteric or out of reach. Whatever your current stage of business growth, embracing this approach is a decision to uplift your brand and secure its place in the hearts—and wallets—of your customers. This chapter is an invitation: adopt these actionable steps, refine your automation systems, and watch as your community thrives, bound together by the very human principles of care and connection.

Creating a highly efficient and nurturing sales and marketing automation system requires a deep understanding of the significance of nurturing automation and heart-centered marketing. These two elements are the backbone of a system that not only efficiently scales a business but also maintains a genuine connection with the audience. Nurturing automation involves the use of automated processes to build, foster, and maintain relationships with potential and existing customers, while heart-centered marketing focuses on approaching marketing and sales strategies with empathy, authenticity, and genuine care for the audience.

Nurturing automation is crucial because it allows businesses to provide personalized experiences to their audience at scale. **By automating personalized interactions**, businesses can reach a wider audience while still making each individual feel valued and understood. This leads to increased customer satisfaction, loyalty, and ultimately, higher conversion rates. Additionally, nurturing automation helps businesses stay top-of-mind with their audience, whether it's through targeted email campaigns, personalized content recommendations, or automated follow-ups based on customer behavior.

Heart-centered marketing complements nurturing automation by infusing the entire customer journey with authenticity and empathy. **Approaching marketing and sales from a heart-centered perspective** means genuinely caring about the needs and feelings of the audience. It involves creating content and messaging that resonates on an emotional level, prioritizing transparency in business practices, and building trust through meaningful interactions. Heart-centered marketing is not just about making a sale; it's about creating a positive impact on the lives of the audience.

When these two elements are combined, they create a powerful system that has the potential to transform businesses. A nurturing automation system that is underpinned by heart-centered marketing builds a loyal community of engaged customers who not only buy from the business but also advocate for it. This community forms the foundation for sustainable growth, as loyal customers not only generate repeat business but also serve as ambassadors for the brand, attracting new customers through word-of-mouth referrals.

Understanding the significance of nurturing automation and heart-centered marketing is pivotal for anyone looking to build a highly efficient and nurturing sales and marketing automation system. It's the synergy between these two elements that drives the success of the system. In the next section, we'll delve into the practical strategies for maintaining a genuine connection with the audience while scaling the business through nurturing automation, shedding light on actionable steps to implement these concepts effectively.

Now, let's explore how to maintain a genuine connection with the audience while scaling the business through nurturing automation.

The heart of your business lies in your ability to maintain a genuine connection with your audience, even as you scale your operations through nurturing automation. While it can be tempting to focus solely on growth and automation, it's crucial to remember that your audience consists of real people with real needs, desires, and emotions. By recognizing the significance of nurturing automation and implementing heart-centered marketing strategies, you can ensure that your business remains deeply connected to your audience, fostering loyalty and trust.

To maintain a genuine connection with your audience while scaling your business, **consistency** is key. Your audience craves reliability and dependability, so ensure that your messaging and interactions with them are consistent across all touchpoints. Whether it's through emails, social media posts, or customer service interactions, your brand voice and values should remain unwavering, reinforcing the authenticity of your connection with your audience.

At the core of maintaining a genuine connection is the practice of **active listening**. Take the time to truly understand the needs and feedback of your audience. Utilize surveys, polls, and feedback forms to gather insights into their preferences and challenges. By demonstrating that you value their opinions and are actively working to address their concerns, you build a deeper sense of trust and rapport.

Personalization is another vital element in maintaining a genuine connection with your audience. Use data-driven insights to tailor your communications and offerings to the specific needs and preferences of different segments of your audience. Whether it's addressing them by name in emails, recommending products based on their purchase history, or acknowledging important milestones in their lives, personalized interactions demonstrate that you see them as individuals, not just numbers in a database.

Finally, **authentic storytelling** can significantly strengthen your connection with your audience. Share your brand's journey, values, and the impact you've had on your customers in a sincere and relatable manner. Incorporate customer testimonials and success stories to showcase how your products or services have positively impacted real people's lives. Authentic storytelling fosters a sense of emotional connection and community, deepening the bond between your audience and your brand.

By upholding these principles of consistency, active listening, personalization, and authentic storytelling, you can create a nurturing environment for your audience even as you scale your business through automation. It's essential to remember that behind every click, open, and purchase is a real person seeking value, connection, and trust. Embracing heart-centered marketing ensures that your growth doesn't come at the expense of the genuine connection you've worked so hard to build.

Harnessing the Power of Segmentation

Segmentation is core to a nurturing automation system, allowing you to customize communication based on where your customers are in their journey. Imagine you're at a dinner party; you wouldn't offer desserts before the main course. In the same vein, segmentation ensures that your messages are **relevant and timely**. Start by categorizing your audience based on their behavior, interests, and past purchases. With these insights, you can tailor email sequences, content delivery, and offers that resonate deeply with each group. This isn't just efficient; it's respectful of your audience's unique needs and positions your business as empathetic and attentive.

Streamlining with Integration

Your sales and marketing tools should work in concert like a symphony, not in isolation. Integrate your CRM, email marketing software, and analytics platforms to build a robust nurturing automation system. This integration **allows for a smooth flow of information**, empowering you to act on data-driven insights. When a potential customer fills out a contact form, for instance, their information should automatically populate in your CRM, triggering a series of personalized follow-ups. By doing so, you remove manual errors and speed up response times, increasing conversion rates while freeing your team to focus on higher-level strategies.

Implementing Behavioral Triggers

Responsive automation is the bridge between observing customer behavior and acting on it. **Behavioral triggers**—like website visits, email opens, or downloads—are your cue to send a tailored message or offer. These triggers should be set up to reflect a customer's interest level, moving them smoothly along the sales funnel. An abandoned cart, for example, could trigger a reminder email with a small discount to encourage a purchase. Behavioral triggers ensure your business is responsive and attentive, operating on *customer time* rather than *company time*.

Timing for Optimal Engagement

Crafting the perfect message isn't enough if it's delivered at the wrong time. **Timing is crucial**; your automation system should include tools that analyze the best times to reach out to your audience. By leveraging AI and machine learning, your system can predict and enact optimal send-times, increasing the likelihood that your messages will be opened and acted upon. This strategy respects your customers' schedules and avoids the perception of your messages as intrusive. Remember, it's not just about when you want to reach out, but when your audience is most receptive.

Dynamic Content for Personalization

Dynamic content takes personalization to a whole new level. Elements like name personalization in emails are just the start; *dynamic content adapts what the viewer sees* based on their preferences and behaviors. For example, return visitors to your website could see a custom welcome message or curated product recommendations. Through automation, create multiple versions of emails and landing pages that speak directly to an individual's needs. **Rich personalization** not only delights but also demonstrates that you view your customers as individuals, not just numbers.

Test, Analyze, and Optimize

Continuous improvement is the lifeblood of an efficient nurturing automation system. Implement A/B testing on your emails, landing pages, and automated sequences to understand what works best. Collect and analyze data on open rates, click-through rates, and conversion metrics to get a clear picture of your performance. This data not only guides you in optimizing your current processes but also helps in **making informed decisions** for future strategies. Remember, an automation system that isn't regularly reviewed and improved upon will stagnate, so keep your approach as dynamic as your content.

Educate Before You Sell

A nurturing automation system is not just about selling; it's a platform for education and adding value to your customers' lives. By providing informative content that solves problems or enhances knowledge, you establish your brand as a **trusted resource**. Automated follow-up sequences can be designed to deliver whitepapers, e-books, or tutorial videos to prospects that have expressed interest in certain topics. Such valuable content generates goodwill and thought leadership, ultimately leading to more informed and eager buyers.

Consistent, Not Constant

Be consistent, but not overbearing with your outreach. Your automation system should be configured to maintain a presence in your customers' lives, but without overwhelming them with frequent contacts. This balance is key to keeping your brand top-of-mind without risking email fatigue or, worse, annoyance. Align communications with your audience's typical engagement patterns, and allow for occasional silence to give them space. The best relationships, including customer relationships, are those where each interaction is anticipated, not dreaded.

Creating a highly efficient and nurturing sales and marketing automation system is a strategic process that requires careful planning and execution. As you implement these strategies, you'll foster a more profound connection with your audience and watch as this connection translates into sustainable business growth. Automation and personalization go hand-in-hand, transforming how you interact with your customers and how they perceive your brand. With dedication and the right approach, your business can thrive by leveraging technology while keeping the human touch at its core.

Now that you understand the significance of nurturing automation and heart-centered marketing for efficiently scaling your business, it's time to put these strategies into action. By maintaining a genuine connection with your audience while scaling your business through nurturing automation, you'll build a loyal community of engaged customers without losing the personal touch.

Remember, the combination of nurturing automation and heart-centered marketing leads to a system that efficiently scales your business while maintaining a genuine connection with your audience. This approach will result in sustainable growth and a loyal community of engaged customers.

As you move forward, keep in mind the strategies for creating a highly efficient and nurturing sales and marketing automation system. It's essential to constantly evaluate and fine-tune your automation processes to ensure that they align with your heart-centered approach. Always prioritize delivering value and building relationships over simply making sales. By doing so, you'll not only scale your business efficiently but also create a thriving and engaged community.

By implementing these practices, you'll be on your way to building an automated empire that is both efficient and genuinely nurturing.

Chapter 10: Empowering Business Growth with the Right Skills and Strategies

"Automation doesn't replace the human element; it augments it, allowing businesses to challen their efforts into creative, empathetic, and ultimately more rewarding endeavors."

A soft glow began to break over the skyline of the industrious city, casting long shadows that played among the sparse trees lining the office complex. Inside, nestled within sleek glass walls and the hum of electronics, Eva grappled with the pressing tide of scalability that threatened the very ethos of her business. Alone in her office, her gaze lingered on a photo of early days, a token of grassroots beginnings and personal connections now at odds with her enterprise's burgeoning demands.

The constant influx of customers once felt like a triumph, but now, the weight of sustaining intimacy in every transaction loomed large. Eva had spent years building a loyal community; their very growth now seemed an adversary to the personal touch she prized. *Can I really preserve this connection we're known for, even as the numbers grow?* she wondered.

Eva caught the reflection of her team in a nearby monitor, aglow with camaraderie and a paralleled concern. They were committed to the vision, to sustainably grow without becoming just another faceless entity. The answer, she knew, nestled in the convergence of heart-centered marketing and nurturing automation. Yet, was the implementation as seamless as the concept?

Her thoughts were punctured by a symphony of keyboard clicks. Looking up, she saw Nathan, her newly hired operations manager, focusing intently on streamlining customer service with an automation tool. It was the harmonious blending of innovation and innate human understanding that she sought. A blend that he, too, sought to perfect under her guidance.

What if they could engineer the very mechanisms that allowed them to shower attention onto their customers without losing the rhythm that made their business dance? The question echoed around the room, resonating against the tangible anxiety of unfaced challenges. Could it be that the same technology threatening to depersonalize their business could also be their most intimate ally?

As day bled into the dusky hues of evening, Eva remained perched, caught in a curious balance between evolving demand and steadfast philosophy. Each strategic plan they considered seemed a step away from the core of their brand. Yet, without evolution, would not stagnation follow? Is there a way to hold the hands of many, without loosening the grasp on the heart that kept a business beating?

Unleashing the Power of Human Touch in a World of Automation

Gone are the days when business growth and automation were viewed as impersonal cogs in an industrial machine. The era of heart-centered marketing beckons, where technology and empathy amalgamate, creating an enviable symbiosis that promises exponential business growth. At the heart of this transformation are the skills and strategies that empower entrepreneurs and companies to embrace automation without losing the soul of customer interaction. The mastery of such tools doesn't just enhance business; it magnifies the quality of each customer relationship.

Cutting-edge automation combined with a nurturing touch is not just a lofty ideal, but a concrete strategy with measurable outcomes.

Businesses now have the unprecedented ability to scale new heights while maintaining the personal connections that distinguish brands in a crowded marketplace. The tools and methods outlined here are transformative, turning indifferent transactions into meaningful engagements, fostering sustainable growth, and building a loyal community.

Acquiring the right skills becomes a pivotal step in this journey. It's about learning how to let machines carry out tasks, freeing up precious human energy for areas where it counts most – fostering relationships. The result? A seamless machine-human collaboration that elevates the customer experience. Automation doesn't replace the human element; it **augments it**, allowing businesses to channel their efforts into creative, empathetic, and ultimately more rewarding endeavors.

The path to scaling your business, with the personal touch intact, involves harnessing the art of delegation. It enables leaders to focus on core competencies, leaving the digestible, repetitive tasks to automation tools designed to execute with precision. **Delegation, when done right, ensures that the human essence of your brand not only remains but flourishes**. Every interaction, automated or not, feels considered, warm, and unmistakably human.

At the core of this chapter lie tactics that have been tried, tested, and proven. These are tools that entrepreneurs and leaders across industries swear by – practices that have propelled small enterprises into the realm of major players, all without losing the sparkle that made them special in the first place. **Sustainable growth and customer loyalty** aren't happy accidents; they're the byproducts of strategic planning, skill development, and the judicious use of marketing automation.

By integrating these insights, businesses stand to gain a competitive advantage in an increasingly automated world. The strategies discussed here are not just about surviving the impersonal onslaught of digital transformation; they are about thriving within it. **Building an engaged community** of customers is about striking the right chord with heart-centered marketing strategies that celebrate the individual while reaching the masses.

As we approach the final act of "Automated Business Empire", we assemble the mosaic of insights shared throughout the book. The journey has revealed the balance between nurturing automation with the finesse of a gardener tending to their garden, to heart-centered marketing that resonates like a finely played melody. This chapter not only cements those concepts into solid, actionable strategies but also threads them into the fabric of everyday business operations, making them an indelible part of a grand entrepreneurial adventure. Here, you craft not only a company but a community, fortified by skills and strategies that align with the beating heart of your business' intent and purpose.

In today's competitive business landscape, the right skills and strategies are crucial to empower businesses to implement nurturing automation and heart-centered marketing. With the right approach, businesses can find the balance between efficiency and personal touch, leading to sustainable growth and a loyal community of engaged customers. Understanding how the right skills and strategies come into play is essential for businesses looking to scale and thrive in the digital age.

First and foremost, understanding the tools and technologies available for nurturing automation is key. The right skills involve mastering marketing automation platforms, customer relationship management (CRM) systems, and email marketing software. These tools, when wielded with expertise, can streamline workflows, personalize customer interactions, and nurture leads, all while maintaining the personal touch that sets a business apart.

Additionally, having a strategic approach to heart-centered marketing can transform the way a business builds relationships with its audience. Techniques like storytelling, empathetic content creation, and community engagement are skills that, when honed, can deeply resonate with customers, fostering a sense of connection and trust. This approach requires a keen understanding of human psychology and emotional resonance in marketing, making it a vital skill for businesses seeking to truly connect with their audience.

Furthermore, the art of balancing automation and personal touch requires strategic planning and execution. It's not just about adopting the latest technology; it's about integrating it seamlessly with an authentic, human-centered approach. Businesses need the skill to create automated systems that feel personal and nurturing, ensuring that customers never feel like just another data point in a system.

While these skills and strategies may seem complex, they are attainable through strategic learning and implementation. Business growth through nurturing automation and heart-centered marketing is not just a lofty goal but an achievable reality for those who possess the right skills and strategies. By leveraging these essential tools, businesses can experience exponential growth while continuing to resonate with their audience on a personal level.

Now, let's explore how to successfully scale a business while maintaining a personal touch through automation and delegation.

Scaling a business while maintaining a personal touch is not just a dream; it's very achievable with the right skills, tactics, and strategies in place. The key to success lies in effectively leveraging automation and delegation to create a highly efficient and nurturing system. This requires careful planning and an understanding of how to execute these elements with a personal touch. Let's delve into the essential steps to successfully scale your business while preserving the valuable connection with your audience.

Start with Strategic Delegation

Delegating tasks is essential for freeing up your time to focus on the critical aspects of your business. Identify the tasks that can be effectively handled by others and trust your team to take them on. This will not only allow you to dedicate more time to nurturing the personal connections with your audience but also empower your team to grow alongside your business.

Implement Nurturing Automation

Utilize marketing automation to maintain a personal touch with your audience at scale. Crafting personalized, automated messages can create a sense of individualized attention. Tailor your automated communications to reflect the values and voice of your brand, ensuring that your audience feels connected at every touchpoint.

Strive for Efficiency Without Compromise

Efficiency is essential, but it should not come at the cost of personalization. Ensure that the systems and processes you implement bring value to your audience and enhance their experience. Automation should aim to streamline operations while enhancing the personal connection, not replacing it.

Empower Your Team with the Right Skills

Invest in training and mentorship to equip your team with the skills they need to maintain a personal touch in their interactions. Emphasize the importance of empathy, active listening, and genuine care in all customer interactions. These skills are foundational in creating an environment where your team can confidently maintain personal relationships while the business scales.

Embrace Change and Innovation

Welcome new technologies and methodologies that can bolster your ability to nurture personal connections. Stay updated on industry trends and best practices, and be willing to adapt and evolve your strategies to meet the changing needs of your audience.

Consistency is Key

Maintain consistency in your messaging and the quality of your interactions. Whether it's in-person engagements or automated communications, ensure that your brand voice and values remain consistent. Consistency fosters trust and loyalty, essential components for maintaining a personal touch as your business expands.

Measure, Adjust, and Refine

Regularly evaluate the impact of your scaling efforts on the personal connection with your audience. Use data to guide your decisions and make adjustments to your strategies as needed. The ability to pivot and refine your approach is critical to sustaining a personal touch throughout the growth of your business.

By adopting these strategies and skills, you can successfully scale your business without sacrificing the personal touch that is so vital to nurturing a loyal community of engaged customers. Balancing automation and delegation with a heartfelt, personal approach is the key to building a thriving business that resonates with your audience on a deeper level.

Harnessing the Community Engagement Model

The modern marketplace is a playground for connectivity and shared experiences. Businesses can no longer rely solely on transactions; they must cultivate relationships and foster loyalty. The Community Engagement Model provides a quintessential framework for nurturing these vital connections. Understanding and implementing this model equips businesses with the ability to create a thriving ecosystem around their brand, enabling both growth and an enduring touchstone of personal interaction.

Community Building: Laying the Foundations

Establishing a community begins with defining its very core - its purpose, values, and guiding principles. This foundational stage is akin to constructing a house; without a solid base, the structure is likely to falter. To forge a strong community, communication channels must be set up effectively, fostering an atmosphere that is not only welcoming but also conducive to active participation. Cohesion is key here, as consistency in message and intent fortifies the community's framework and prepares it for sustainable expansion.

Creating a sense of belonging among community members accelerates involvement and fuels the collective energy of the group. This isn't just about membership numbers; it's about each individual feeling valued and understood. Encourage early interaction and dialogue to set the tone, making it clear that every voice within the community has the power to resonate and be heard.

Content Creation and Curation: Nourishing the Community

Once the groundwork is laid, it's time for the community to take shape with content that connects and captivates. Consider this stage as nurturing your garden; your content must be the sunlight and water that help your community flourish. Identifying the right content formats and topics, aligning with the interests and needs of your community, is vital. Content should not only inform and entertain but also invite contributions from the members themselves, transforming passive consumers into active participants.

Establish a rhythm through a regular publishing schedule that community members can anticipate and look forward to. This reliability fosters trust and and solidifies their engagement. Regular, quality content acts as the heartbeat of the community, keeping it alive and vibrant.

Community Engagement: The Art of Connection

Fostering engagement is an active, ongoing process requiring attention and energy. Consider this stage the nurturing of your social fabric, weaving together the threads of individual members to form a cohesive, robust network. Lead by example with active community moderation, initiate discussions that stimulate thought and interaction, and organize virtual events where members can interact and bond over shared experiences.

Facilitation is key—provide platforms for members to network, collaborate, and forge relationships beyond the confines of structured events. Recognition and encouragement are powerful tools; they validate contributions and spur further involvement. The strength of a community lies in its members' sense of investment and ownership; therefore, encouraging a collaborative spirit is instrumental for vibrant engagement.

Community Growth and Advocacy: Cultivating Loyalty

The final stage of the model revolves around expansion and empowering your community to be the voice of your brand. Recognizing and rewarding active members not only bolsters their loyalty but also incentivizes them to become brand advocates.

Implementing referral programs can turn satisfied customers into potent ambassadors, extending your reach organically.

Encourage and highlight members' experiences and successes. By celebrating these stories, you signal to the community an appreciation for their input, and you showcase tangible benefits of being an active community member. This sense of shared triumph not only inspires existing members but also intrigues and attracts new ones, perpetuating the cycle of growth and advocacy.

Through the deliberate and strategic application of the Community Engagement Model, you lay the blueprint for a self-sustaining ecosystem that not only champions your brand but also adds intrinsic value to both the business and its dedicated followers. By fostering a transparent, collaborative, and rewarding environment, customers transform into a close-knit community of champions, supporting the business through thick and thin.

This approach is not a one-size-fits-all solution but a flexible framework that adapts over time and across contexts. As the needs and dynamics of your community evolve, so should the strategies you employ within this model. By continuously refining and adapting to the rhythms of your community, your efforts will not only lead to success in the present but will pave the way for innovation and growth in the future.

In the tapestry of business growth, the Community Engagement Model represents the vibrant strands that hold the fabric together, ensuring that each thread contributes to a larger, beautiful design. With the right skills and a strategic approach, businesses can harness this model to achieve sustainable growth while keeping the pulse of personal touch beating strong at the heart of their community.

With the right skills and strategies in place, you now hold the power to transform your business. You have learned how to effectively scale your business while maintaining a personal touch through strategic automation and delegation. As a result, you are equipped to foster sustainable growth and build a loyal community of engaged customers without sacrificing the personal touch.

By understanding how the right skills and strategies empower businesses to implement nurturing automation and heart-centered marketing, you have gained a powerful advantage in the competitive world of business. You now have the tools to create a thriving community and scale your business while preserving the genuine connection and care that your customers deserve.

Remember, success is not a matter of chance, but a matter of choice. It's about the deliberate actions you take, the skills you develop, and the strategies you implement. By choosing to embrace the knowledge and insights shared in this book, you are setting yourself up for an exciting journey toward business growth, impact, and influence.

As you move forward, focus on applying these insights in practical ways. Blend your newfound skills with actionable tactics, and measure your progress as you pave the way for substantial growth and a lasting impact. You have the potential to build an empire that is both efficient and nurturing, and it all starts with the skills and strategies you've acquired.

Embrace the journey, knowing that every step you take will bring you closer to your vision. Your commitment to learning, implementing, and adapting will make all the difference. Stand firm in your resolve, and let your business flourish with heart-centered marketing and nurturing automation – for that is the path to creating an empire that is both massively successful and deeply connected.

Embracing the Future with Humanity at the Heart of Automation

As we draw the final curtain on our exploration of how to intertwine the seamlessness of automation with the genuine connection of human interaction, it's time to reflect on how we, as business leaders and visionaries, can carry these lessons forward. The landscape of business is a dynamic tapestry, continuously evolving with technological innovations and the ever-changing needs of our customers. Yet, amid this perpetual change lies an immutable truth—our success hinges on our ability to foster genuine relationships and communities.

The real-world applications of the insights presented in these pages are vast and varied. Whether you're a solopreneur seeking to make your first hire or a seasoned executive steering your company into a new era of growth, the principles of heart-centered marketing will serve as your compass. Within your grasp is a blueprint for creating systems that captivate your audience at scale while holding fast to the personal touch that defines exceptional brands.

In recapping the key takeaways, remember the importance of **designing automation with empathy**, ensuring that every automated touchpoint feels as warm and personalized as a handwritten note. We delved into the power of storytelling, nurturing funnels that guide with care, and the art of community-building that turns customers into passionate advocates. Each chapter served as a stepping stone toward the final goal: A thriving, engaged, and loyal community.

To put these lessons into action requires commitment and refinement. Start small, perhaps by automating a single customer journey, gauging its effectiveness, and refining it with a blend of analytics and heart. Gradually expand your automated systems, always with an ear to the ground, listening and adapting to the voices of your community.

This journey isn't without its limitations. Technology can falter, and human behavior can be unpredictable; still, these are not roadblocks but opportunities for creativity and growth. As I have shared from my own experiences and the successes of professionals worldwide, the unforeseen challenges often pave the way for the most innovative solutions.

Take courage in knowing you're not alone on this path. The community you are building starts with you, but it includes every connection you've made along the way. Reach out, collaborate, share experiences, and grow together.

In closing, I implore you to take that **bold step into the future** where efficiency and empathy coexist harmoniously. Use the knowledge you've gained here not just as a strategy, but as a philosophy woven through every fiber of your business. Remember, the technology is at your command, and when guided by a heart-centric approach, it can become your greatest ally in achieving the extraordinary.

Let's leave with a thought that encapsulates this journey—one that should linger in your mind and propel you forward with determination:

"Technology is best when it brings people together." – Matt Mullenweg

With that, step out and craft your automated empire, one that is vast, efficient, and, above all, profoundly human.

Resources

Consultation

If you want to book a consultation with me to discuss your company's automation needs, please complete the following application: https://bit.ly/ABEconsult

Course

If you want the course that accompanies this book, please use the following link. While the course is $997, because you purchased this book you can get the course for $97 Use the promo code **ABEBOOK** https://bit.ly/ABEFundamentals

My Tech Stack

I am often asked to share my tech stack in my business. I can tell you that Keap is at the core. To know my entire tech stack, jump into the fundamentals course for full current list.

Keap - Positioned at the core of my tech arsenal, Keap seamlessly embodies the principles outlined in this book. This platform, tailored for data-driven individuals deciphering human behavior, is pivotal. For those aiming to nurture audiences, leads, and customers at every touchpoint, Keap stands out. Access my exclusive pricing below, substantially lower than the standard rates on their website. Additionally, signing up through my links grants you complimentary entry into my Automation Inner Circle – a $497 monthly value as of this book's writing. Why the generosity? Because my genuine goal is to aid you in cultivating a thriving automated business empire, and I'm here to

support your journey.
Keap Pro - https://bit.ly/ABEKeappro

Keap Max - https://bit.ly/ABEKeapMax

Keap Ultimate - https://bit.ly/ABEKeapUltimate

Glossary of Terms

This is a glossary of terms that I might have used in this book. Since many of these terms are now second nature to me, I wanted to make sure I gave you a clear understanding.

Automation:

- The process of using technology and software to perform repetitive tasks, streamline workflows, and optimize business processes without constant manual intervention.

CRM (Customer Relationship Management):

- A system for managing a company's interactions with current and future customers, typically involving data analysis to improve business relationships.

Lead Generation:

- The process of attracting and converting potential customers into leads, often through various marketing strategies and tactics.

Funnel:

- A visual representation of the customer journey, illustrating the steps from initial awareness to conversion, typically used in sales and marketing.

Segmentation:

- Dividing a target market into specific groups based on

demographics, behavior, or other criteria to tailor marketing efforts and communication.

Personalization:

- Tailoring marketing messages and experiences to individual preferences and behaviors, enhancing the connection with the audience.

Drip Campaign:

- A series of automated, scheduled messages delivered to prospects or customers over time, designed to nurture relationships and guide them through the sales funnel.

Heart-Centered Marketing:

- An approach to marketing that prioritizes authenticity, empathy, and genuine connection, focusing on building relationships and trust rather than just transactions.

Empathy Mapping:

- A technique used in marketing to understand and visualize the emotions, thoughts, and behaviors of a target audience, fostering more empathetic communication.

Community Building:

- The strategic process of cultivating a loyal and engaged community around a brand or business through shared values, content, and interactions.

Content Marketing:

- A marketing strategy focused on creating and distributing valuable, relevant content to attract and engage a target audience, often as a means of building brand authority.

KPIs (Key Performance Indicators):

- Measurable metrics used to evaluate the success of marketing and sales efforts, providing insights into performance and areas for improvement.

Conversion Rate:
- The percentage of website visitors or leads that take a desired action, such as making a purchase or filling out a form.

Retargeting:

- Displaying targeted ads to individuals who have previously interacted with a website or engaged with certain content, aiming to re-engage and convert them.

Authenticity:

- The quality of being genuine and true to oneself, a crucial element in building trust and credibility in heart-centered marketing.

Dynamic Content:

- Content that is personalized and changes based on user behavior, preferences, or demographic information, providing a tailored experience.

Customer Persona:

> · A detailed and semi-fictional representation of your ideal customer, incorporating demographics, behaviors, motivations, and goals.

Behavior Tracking:

> · The process of monitoring and analyzing user interactions and behaviors across digital platforms to gain insights into preferences and trends.

Lead Scoring:

> · A method of assigning values to leads based on their behavior, engagement, and demographics, helping prioritize and qualify leads for sales efforts.

Customer Journey:

> · The complete end-to-end experience a customer has with a brand, encompassing every interaction from awareness to post-purchase engagement.

Sales and Marketing Automation:

> · The use of technology and software to automate repetitive tasks in sales and marketing processes, improving efficiency and scalability.

Trigger:

> · A specific event or action that initiates an automated response or workflow within a sales or

marketing automation system.

A/B Testing:

·   The practice of comparing two versions (A and B) of a webpage, email, or other marketing asset to determine which performs better in terms of user engagement or conversion.

Multi-channel Marketing:

·   The use of multiple channels (e.g., social media, email, website) to reach and engage with a target audience, creating a cohesive and integrated marketing strategy.

Upselling:

·   The technique of encouraging customers to purchase a more expensive or upgraded product or service, increasing the average transaction value.

Lead Nurturing:

·   The process of building and maintaining relationships with leads over time through targeted and personalized communication, with the goal of converting them into customers.

Inbound Marketing:

·   A marketing approach focused on creating valuable content and experiences to attract and engage prospects, aligning with the buyer's journey.

Retention Rate:

· The percentage of customers or subscribers who continue to use a product or service over a specific period, indicating customer loyalty and satisfaction.

Churn Rate:

· The rate at which customers or subscribers stop using a product or service, reflecting customer attrition.

9 780990 574224